CONTENTS

CINNAMON ROLL MILKSHAKE
BY MOLLY HARBRIDGE. RECIPE ON PAGE 75.

WITH SYRUP AND CARAMEL SAUCE

FORWARD

An Introduction from Chef Thom England, Culinary Instructor at Ivy Tech Community College

Personally, I am inspired when I see students smile after making a perfect dish. I am inspired to share the happy thoughts conjured by the artistry of food. I am inspired when I walk by a class in lecture and see all the faces of the students mesmerized by the science of cooking. I am inspired when I read Michael Pollen describe the food systems in the United States. Inspired to lead change. I am inspired by the tomatoes hanging on a plant in August. Inspired to teach others what good food is. I am inspired by my travels. Inspired to teach others what it means to be hospitable.

In class we often talk about how eating fresh, local and seasonal foods produces the best flavors. We look at what Alice Waters did on the West Coast, taking French cuisine and using local ingredients instead of importing foods from halfway around the world. Others have done this as well, and they are the ones that have created what we call "New American cuisine".

We offer a class at Ivy Tech Community College that studies the history of American regional cuisine. Many times, students will comment on how they like certain parts of the recipe but the ingredients are outside of the Midwestern palate or general availability. Working on *Indiana Harvest* gave us the perfect opportunity to play with classics from around the United States and convert them into Midwestern adaptations.

Students were encouraged to submit up to three recipes from each of the American regions covered in the class:

New England, Mid-Atlantic, Southern, Floribbean, Cajun/Creole, Tex/Mex, Southwest and Rockies, California, Pacific Northwest, and Hawaii. I thought this would get them talking about how the other regions of the U.S. eat. But instead, they were engrossed in learning what grew in the Midwest. We have gotten into the "world is flat" syndrome in the way we eat. We now find things in the store that are available year-round even though they are only ripe in the Midwest for a couple of months out of the year. This project showcased what is available in Indiana throughout the seasons. The students were thrilled to find things like persimmons and pawpaws and bring them in for the class to try.

The week before I unveiled this project to the students, I had dinner at a local restaurant. I glanced through the menu and saw a dose of inspiration. They were serving a Chicken-Fried Crab Cake. It was a perfect example of what we were looking for. They served it with a sauce made from local produce which made it familiar to the local consumer.

Corn is king in Indiana. And not just the commercial crops we drive by every day. I think most people that have grown up in Indiana will have a story about eating the perfect ear of yellow corn. Then, there is the tomato. And the great beef. I think one dish that would showcase it all is a grilled steak with a corn salsa. From this book, I hope readers get enjoyment out of cooking and eating the foods, but more importantly, I hope they renew some traditions of using local foods. I have included a few introductory sentences with each recipe to further explain the students' visions and tempt the home chef. Enjoy!

GOING FOR THE FRENCH EXPERIENCE

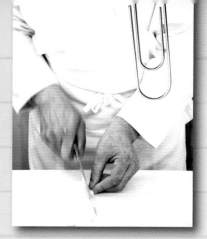

APPETIZERS

At 57 years old, Georgia-born student Hollis Joseph Thomas has been taking classes at Ivy Tech Community College for the past 10 years. Two years ago he decided to take courses toward a culinary major in the hospitality administration program, a degree he will recieve when he graduates in 2010.

"I picked Ivy Tech for the accreditation, cost of classes and talented and experienced culinary staff," he says. Thomas, whose wife works at the college, will further enrich his experience with an educational venture to France with the Study Abroad program in the spring of 2009.

"The frequency and flexibility of the courses offered is very appealing, and each of the instructors brings their own strengths and specialties. We can all continue to learn from them even after we graduate."

Thomas

JAMIE MARKS
HOMETOWN: MOORESVILLE. INDIANA

COOKING A CREEKSIDE DELICACY.

CHUNKY CRAWFISH SPREAD

BY JAMIE MARKS
(PICTURED ON OPPOSITE PAGE)

I REMEMBER CATCHING CRAWFISH as a kid in the stream that ran behind our house. We never really knew you could eat them, but now I know they are a delicacy. When combined with this wonderful blue cheese from the Midwest, this recipe is heavenly.

1 16-ounce package frozen cooked crawfish tails, thawed, peeled and deveined
1 8-ounce package cream cheese, softened
¼ cup Maytag Blue Cheese
1 medium green bell pepper, finely chopped
1 medium sweet red bell pepper, finely chopped
1 small onion, finely chopped
6 cloves garlic, minced
½ teaspoon Creole seasoning
½ teaspoon kosher salt
6-12 drops hot sauce
Assorted crackers, to serve

1. On a cutting board, chop the crawfish. Pat dry.
2. In a small mixing bowl, beat together the cream cheese and blue cheese until well combined. Add in the peppers, onion, garlic, Creole seasoning, salt and hot sauce.
3. Stir in the chopped crawfish. Cover and refrigerate for at least 2 hours.
4. Serve the chilled spread with assorted crackers.

MAKES 3 CUPS

WHITE SANGRIA

BY JAMIE MARKS

THIS IS A SPRINGTIME FAVORITE; as the cherries ripen on the Midwest trees and the citrus is coming up from Florida. Just sit back and drink a couple glasses while contemplating the coming summer.

2 cups lemon-flavored club soda, chilled
1½ cups dry white wine, chilled
¼ cup orange liqueur
¼ cup vodka
¼ cup lime juice
1 tablespoon sugar
1 small orange, cut into 8 slices
1 small apple, cored and cut into 8 wedges
1 lemon, cut into 8 slices
¼ cup Montmorency cherries
Ice cubes, as needed

1. In a 2-quart pitcher or punch bowl, combine the club soda, wine, orange liqueur, vodka, lime juice and sugar. Stir until the sugar is completely dissolved.
2. Add oranges, apples, lemons and cherries and stir well to combine.
3. To serve, fill 8 12-ounce glasses with ice cubes. Transfer 1 orange slice, 1 apple wedge, 1 lemon slice and 2 cherries from the punch bowl or pitcher into each glass and top with ½ cup sangria.

SERVES 4

JOEL RIFKIND, DDS
HOMETOWN: INDIANAPOLIS, INDIANA

A TRIBUTE TO SUMMER'S STAPLES.

HOOSIER FRUIT SALSA

BY JOEL RIFKIND, DDS
(PICTURED ON OPPOSITE PAGE)

THIS RECIPE IS GREAT IN THE LATE SUMMER, when the Indiana melons produce that wonderful sweet smell in the air.

½ cup ¼-inch-dice honeydew melon
½ cup orange segments
½ cup ¼-inch-dice pineapple
½ cup diced cantaloupe
½ cup halved seedless green grapes
¼ cup ¼-inch-dice red bell pepper
1 teaspoon seeded, minced jalapeño pepper
¼ cup minced red onion
¼ cup balsamic vinegar
1 tablespoon chopped fresh cilantro
Kosher salt and freshly ground black pepper,
  to taste
Tortilla chips, to serve

1. In a bowl, combine the honeydew, orange, pineapple, cantaloupe, grapes, bell pepper, jalapeño and red onion.
2. Stir in the vinegar, cilantro and salt and pepper, to taste.
3. Place the salsa in a small bowl and serve immediately with tortilla chips. If you are making this ahead of time, chill until service.

SERVES 4

CHORIZO AND MOREL TAPAS

BY DARCY SMINK
(PICTURED ON OPPOSITE PAGE)

IN THE EARLY SPRING HOOSIERS SCOUR THE COUNTRYSIDE in search of the earthy morel mushroom. This recipe combines the heavy flavor with the spices of the Southwest to produce a great little treat.

1 pound Spanish chorizo, casing intact
2 tablespoons olive oil
24 morel mushrooms, cleaned
3 Anaheim chilies, roasted, peeled and cut into
  1-inch pieces*

1. Leaving the casing on the chorizo, slice it into ½-inch-thick slices.

2. In a saute pan over medium-high heat, heat the olive oil. Add the chorizo slices and cook, stirring, until they are no longer pink (about 7-8 minutes).

3. Add the mushrooms to the pan and continue to cook for 1-2 minutes, until the mushrooms begin to absorb the fat in the pan.

4. To serve, thread a pepper piece, a slice of chorizo and a morel mushroom onto a 4-inch-long bamboo skewer. Repeat until all the ingredients are used. Serve the skewers hot or at room temperature.

Anaheim chilies are also known as chile verde or New Mexican chilies. To roast them, place them under a hot broiler until they are charred on all sides (about 5-10 minutes). Immediately place them in a bowl and cover with plastic wrap; allow the chilies to steam for 10-15 minutes. Peel and cut as needed.

SERVES 6-8

PAUL ROBINSON
HOMETOWN: LAFAYETTE, INDIANA

MARRYING INDIANA'S FAVORITE CROPS.

PORK, APPLE AND ONION EMPANADAS

BY PAUL ROBINSON
(PICTURED ON OPPOSITE PAGE)

Indiana produces prodigious amounts of both pork and apples. In fact, I believe we produce the nation's best in both categories. When combined in these delicate pastries they become a mouthwatering lunch.

DOUGH

2 cups flour
2 teaspoons baking powder
½ teaspoon kosher salt
2 tablespoons chilled lard*
1 egg, lightly beaten
½ cup milk

FILLING

1 tablespoon butter
1 pound ground pork
1 yellow onion, finely diced
1 Red Delicious apple, finely diced
2 eggs, lightly beaten
½ teaspoon dried thyme
½ teaspoon dried rubbed sage
1 teaspoon caraway seeds
Kosher salt and freshly ground black pepper, to taste
Milk, as needed
Chipotle sour cream† and/or salsa, to serve

1. For the dough, in a large mixing bowl, sift together the flour, baking powder and salt.

2. Add in the chilled lard and mix, using an electric mixer, until well combined.

3. In a separate small bowl, whisk together the egg and the milk. Add to the flour mixture and mix until the dough is well combined and free of lumps.

4. Roll out the dough to ¼-inch thick and cut into pieces 2½ inches in diameter.

5. For the filling, in a pan over medium-high heat, melt the butter. Cook the pork until browned and turn heat down to medium. Add the onion and cook until translucent. Add the apple and cook until the slices are tender. Remove from heat and allow the mixture to cool.

6. Once the pork mixture has cooled, stir in the eggs, thyme, sage, caraway seeds, and salt and pepper, to taste.

7. Preheat oven to 400 degrees.

8. Onto a circle of pastry dough, spoon 1 tablespoon of filling. Fold the pastry dough circle in half over the filling to create a half circle. Seal the edges with a fork and brush the outside with milk. Repeat for the remaining pastry dough circles until all of the empanadas have been filled.

9. Place the filled empanadas on a greased baking sheet and bake in the 400-degree oven for 20 minutes.

10. Serve the warm empanadas with a dollop of chipotle sour cream and/or salsa.

*Lard is an animal-based product. You can substitute the lard with shortening, which is vegetable based.

†To make chipotle sour cream, combine 8 ounces of sour cream with 3 tablespoons of chipotle powder. Mix well.

YIELDS 10-12 EMPANADAS

PORK MEATBALLS IN PILONCILLO-SOUR SAUCE

BY DARCY SMINK
(PICTURED BELOW, LEFT)

OVER THE PAST SEVERAL YEARS PORK has been bred so that the fat content is very low. Now, many times the family recipes for pork won't work without the addition of a little oil. Unfortunately, without the fat the pork is less flavorful. This sauce accents the pork well so that it will enhance the natural qualities of the dish.

MEATBALLS

1 pound ground pork*
1 egg, lightly beaten
1 teaspoon kosher salt
½ teaspoon freshly ground black pepper
3 tablespoons cornflake cereal crumbs
1 small red onion, minced
1 tablespoon soy sauce
3 tablespoons corn oil

PILONCILLO-SOUR SAUCE

2 tablespoons soy sauce
2 tablespoons corn oil
3 tablespoons cider vinegar
2 tablespoons dark (oscuro) piloncillo, softened and chopped†
1 tablespoon tomato paste
1 red bell pepper, coarsely chopped
1 small red onion, coarsely chopped
1 clove garlic, minced
1 teaspoon minced fresh ginger
½ cup pineapple chunks, in juice

1. For the meatballs, in a large bowl, combine the ground pork, egg, salt, pepper, cornflake crumbs, minced red onion and 1 tablespoon of the soy sauce.

2. Using your hands or a meatballer, form the mixture into 1-inch balls.

3. In a large saute pan over medium heat, heat 3 tablespoons of the corn oil. Working in batches, saute the meatballs in the hot corn oil until lightly browned on all sides. Be careful not to crowd the pan.

4. Remove the meatballs to a paper towel-lined plate and drain well.

5. For the piloncillo-sour sauce, in a small bowl, stir together the cider vinegar, piloncillo, 2 tablespoons soy sauce and the tomato paste. Mix until well combined and set aside.

6. In a Dutch oven over medium-high heat, heat the remaining 2 tablespoons corn oil. Add the bell pepper and chopped red onion and saute until softened (about 4 minutes).

7. Add in the garlic and ginger and saute until fragrant (about 2 minutes).

8. Stir in the vinegar-piloncillo mixture from step 5 and bring to a boil. Add in the pineapple chunks and juice and continue to cook until heated through.

9. Reduce the heat to medium-low. Add in the meatballs and stir to combine. Cover and cook until the meatballs are heated through (about 15 minutes).

10. To serve, place the meatballs with the sauce in a large serving bowl and serve with toothpicks or party skewers.

*Chef Smink prefers Royer Farms ground pork.

†Piloncillo is unrefined solid cane sugar, also known as panela or panocha. It is sold in Latino markets and finer grocery stores.

MAKES 20 1-INCH MEATBALLS

INDIANA CORN CAKES
WITH TAMARIND SAUCE

BY DARCY SMINK
(PICTURED BELOW, RIGHT)

THIS RECIPE TAKES THE INDIANA CORN CAKE up a notch with the addition of the tamarind sauce. Tamarind is a tree pod that has a pulp with wonderful flavor. It is the main flavor ingredient in A1 Steak Sauce. Tamarind and sorghum molasses are the perfect complement to one another.

1 tablespoon tamarind paste
½ cup water
2 tablespoons packed dark brown sugar
2 tablespoons sorghum*
1 clove garlic, minced
¼ teaspoon red pepper flakes
1 teaspoon garam masala
5 ears sweet Indiana corn
2 eggs, separated
2 tablespoons all-purpose flour
1 tablespoon sugar
¼ teaspoon kosher salt
¼ teaspoon freshly ground black pepper
2 tablespoons vegetable oil

1. In a saucepan, combine the tamarind paste, water, brown sugar, sorghum, garlic, red pepper flakes and garam masala. Simmer over low heat until the mixture is thick and syrupy, stirring occasionally (about 5 minutes). Remove from heat and allow the sauce to cool to room temperature.

2. While the sauce is cooling, cut the kernels from the ears of corn and place them in a large bowl.

3. Beat the egg yolks slightly, and then add them to the bowl with the corn. Mix them together until they are combined.

4. Stir in the flour, sugar, salt and pepper. Set aside.

5. In the bowl of a stand mixer, beat the egg whites until stiff peaks form. Fold the egg whites into the corn mixture.

6. In a skillet over high heat, heat the vegetable oil.

7. In heaping tablespoonfuls, drop mounds of the corn batter into the hot oil, being careful not to crowd the skillet.

8. Reduce the heat to medium and cook the corn cakes until they are golden brown (about 2-3 minutes). Flip the cakes over and continue to cook until the opposite sides are browned. Continue to cook the corn cakes in batches until all of the batter is used.

9. Serve the cakes immediately, topped with the tamarind sauce.

Chef Smink recommends Gold Run brand sorghum.

SERVES 4

SOUPS AND SALADS

Elise Haskett started at Ivy Tech Community College in the summer of 2008. Already pursuing a degree from the Department of Food Science at Purdue University, Haskett discovered the two colleges collaborated to offer a degree in culinary science. Broadening her existing interest in the field, she decided to take a year to obtain the second degree as well.

Growing up in Seymour, Indiana, Haskett counts her mother as her earliest culinary influence. "I can remember baking cookies with her when I was really young," she says. Those early experiences led Haskett, set to graduate from Purdue University in spring 2011, to pursue a degree in the culinary industry.

As for future Ivy Tech students, the 21 year old has just a few words of advice: "Be focused and ready to learn a lot."

ELISE HASKETT
HOMETOWN: SEYMOUR, INDIANA

A BOWL OF HOOSIER GOLD.

INDIANA SPICY CORN SOUP

BY ELISE HASKETT
(PICTURED ON OPPOSITE PAGE)

For the best results pick and cut the kernels off the cob instead of using bagged kernels. The "milk" of the cob adds richness to the soup and also helps to thicken it.

2 tablespoons unsalted butter
¼ cup ¼-inch-dice red bell pepper
½ cup ½-inch-dice onion
½ cup ½-inch-dice celery
1 cup ¼-inch-dice potato
2 cups peeled, seeded and ½-inch-dice tomatoes*
1½ cup corn kernels
2 cups chicken stock
2 teaspoons Old Bay Seasoning
½ teaspoon kosher salt
¼ teaspoon freshly ground black pepper
¼ teaspoon red pepper flakes
½ cup green peas
1½ teaspoons lemon juice

1. In a pot over medium heat, melt the butter. Add the bell peppers and onions and cook for 4 minutes.

2. Add the celery and cook for 3 minutes.

3. Stir in the potato, tomatoes, corn and chicken stock. Add the Old Bay, salt, pepper and red pepper flakes and bring the soup to a simmer. Allow it to cook for 25 minutes.

4. Add the peas and cook for another 10 minutes.

5. Adjust seasonings, if necessary, and stir in the lemon juice. Serve.

*To peel a tomato, first cut out the stem with a paring knife and then slice a shallow X in the opposite end. Using a slotted spoon, plunge the tomato into boiling water for 2-3 seconds, and then immediately shock it in an ice water bath. Remove the cooled tomato from the ice water and peel.

SERVES 4

KIMBERLY KISER

A VELVETY WINTER WARMER.

WALNUT SOUP

BY KIMBERLY KISER
(PICTURED BELOW)

Black walnuts are prevalent in the Midwest. The Indiana Nut Growers Association is a good place to be able to source most any tree nut or fruit.

WALNUT BUTTER

1½ cups walnuts
1-2 tablespoons olive oil
1-2 teaspoons maple syrup
Pinch-¼ teaspoon salt

1. Preheat oven to 200 degrees.

2. Spread the walnuts on a baking sheet. Bake in the 200-degree oven until the nuts become fragrant (about 5 minutes)

3. Place the walnuts in a bowl of a food processor. Process, and while the motor is running, slowly drizzle in the olive oil 1 teaspoon at a time until the mixture begins to blend together. Stop periodically to scrape down the sides of the bowl.

4. Once the mixture has begun to blend together, with the motor still running, add the syrup and salt, to taste. Start with 1 teaspoon of syrup and a pinch of salt, adding more as needed. Process until the butter is well combined.

SOUP

1 tablespoon canola oil
½ cup sliced mushrooms
2 ribs celery, chopped
1 small onion, chopped
2 carrots, chopped
6 cups vegetable broth
1 cup Walnut Butter
1 teaspoon kosher salt
½ teaspoon cayenne pepper
1 tablespoon freshly squeezed lemon juice
1 carrot, grated, to garnish
¼ cup sour cream, to garnish
2 tablespoons finely chopped fresh chives, to garnish

1. In a large saucepan over medium heat, heat the canola oil. Add the mushrooms and saute until they have softened and released their juices.

2. In a second large saucepan over medium heat, combine the celery, onion, chopped carrots and 3 cups vegetable broth. Bring the mixture to a boil and then reduce to a simmer. Cover and continue to cook for 30 minutes or until the carrots are tender.

3. Transfer the mixture to a food processor or blender and process on high until smooth.

4. Return the mixture to the saucepan and continue to cook over medium-low heat, until it reaches a simmer.

5. Stir in the walnut butter, salt, cayenne pepper and the remaining 3 cups vegetable broth. Return the soup to a simmer.

6. Immediately before serving, stir in the lemon juice. Divide the soup among bowls and garnish with the grated carrots, a dollop of sour cream and the chopped chives.

SERVES 7

THE CURE FOR COLD-WEATHER BLUES.

JOHNATHAN DEMO
HOMETOWN: FLINT, MICHIGAN

MIDWEST TWIST ON A NEW ENGLAND STAPLE.

CORN AND SHRIMP CHOWDER

BY JOHNATHAN DEMO
(PICTURED ON OPPOSITE PAGE)

Corn and shrimp are a perfect collaboration. The flavors of the corn bring out the sweetness in the shrimp.

4 ears corn
3 tablespoons butter
2 scallions, thinly sliced
2 cups chicken stock
Kosher salt and freshly ground white pepper,
   to taste
½ cup heavy cream
1 pound 26-30-size shrimp, tails removed

1. Cut the kernels from the ears of corn; you should have about 2 cups.

2. In a small saucepan over medium heat, melt the butter. Add the scallions and saute until softened (about 3 minutes).

3. Stir in the stock and the corn. Season with salt and white pepper, to taste, and simmer, uncovered, for 10 minutes.

4. Add the cream and stir well. Add the shrimp, and reduce heat to low. Allow the soup to simmer gently, uncovered, until the shrimp turn pink and begin to curl (about 5 minutes). Adjust the seasoning, if needed, and serve.

SERVES 4-6

FRESH FIG AND YOGURT SOUP

BY KIMBERLY KISER
(PICTURED ON PAGE 22)

Sheep's milk has a much smaller fat globule than cow's milk. This will produce yogurt that is silkier. It is easier for people who are lactose intolerant to digest.

2 ½ pounds (about 4 cups) fresh or dried figs
½ cup dates, pitted and chopped
1 quart apple juice*
Kosher salt and freshly ground black pepper,
   to taste
2 teaspoons sugar
1 cup sheep's milk yogurt†

1. Preheat broiler.

2. Wash the figs well and remove any stems. Roughly chop them into quarters, reserving 4 figs (16 quarters) for garnish.

3. Place the figs in the bowl of a food processor and add the apple juice. Puree until the mixture has the consistency of a thick milkshake. Season with salt and pepper, to taste. Place in the refrigerator to chill for 30 minutes.

4. Take the reserved fig quarters and sprinkle the cut sides with the sugar. Place the figs sugared side up in a flameproof baking dish.

5. Broil the fig quarters about 4 inches from the heat until the tops are bubbling and lightly browned (about 3-5 minutes).

6. Divide the chilled soup among 8 cold bowls. Top each bowl with a dollop of fresh yogurt and 2 broiled fig quarters.

*Chef Kiser recommends apple juice from Prairie Moon Orchard, Francesville, Indiana.

†Sheep's milk yogurt should be available at Whole Foods or Fresh Market. If you can not find it, plain yogurt will work.

SERVES 4

BRE EINES
HOMETOWN: INDIANAPOLIS, INDIANA

TRADITIONAL FRUIT GOES TROPICAL.

CARIBBEAN APPLE SALAD

BY BRE EINES
(PICTURED ON OPPOSITE PAGE)

There are more than 20 different apple varieties grown in the Central Indiana region. Just visit your local apple orchard to find the six different varieties for this recipe.

6 apples of different varieties, cored and diced
1 12-ounce can pineapple juice
4 tablespoons sesame seed oil
2 tablespoons apple cider vinegar
2 tablespoons chopped fresh parsley or
   1 tablespoon dried parsley
½ teaspoon fresh rosemary
½ teaspoon lemon pepper
⅛ teaspoon kosher salt

1. Combine all of the ingredients in an airtight container with a lid. Shake vigorously for 30 seconds.
2. Serve immediately.

YIELDS 1½ CUPS; SERVES 6

ONION AND CITRUS SALAD

BY DARCY SMINK
(PICTURED BELOW)

Indiana-grown onions tend to have a spicy heat to them. It is balanced with the citrus in this recipe.

¼ cup extra-virgin olive oil
Juice of 1 lemon
2 teaspoons kosher salt
2 teaspoons freshly ground white pepper
1 large red onion, thinly sliced
2 tablespoons red wine vinegar
Zest of 1 orange
5 navel oranges
1 pink grapefruit
1 tablespoon finely chopped fresh dill

1. In a medium stainless steel bowl, combine 2 tablespoons of the olive oil with the lemon juice and 1 teaspoon each of the salt and pepper. Add the sliced onion to the bowl and toss to coat. Allow the onion to marinate in the oil for 20 minutes at room temperature.
2. Meanwhile, in a second stainless steel bowl, whisk together the remaining olive oil, vinegar, orange zest and the remaining salt and pepper. Set aside.
3. Remove the rind and white membranes from the navel oranges and grapefruit. Cut the citrus into thin slices.
4. Arrange the citrus slices on a large serving platter. Drizzle the dressing on top of the fruit and top with the onion slices. Sprinkle the entire platter with dill and serve immediately.

SERVES 6

AN EYE-CATCHING STARTER.

JOHNATHAN DEMO
HOMETOWN: FLINT. MICHIGAN

SPICED SHRIMP AND ELEGANT GREENS.

MARGARITA SHRIMP SALAD

BY JOHNATHAN DEMO
(PICTURED ON OPPOSITE PAGE)

I love the classic Southwest flavors of this dish. All the vegetables used in this recipe are grown around the Midwest. Serve in a margarita glass for a festive look.

SHRIMP

2 tablespoons chopped fresh cilantro
2 cloves garlic, minced
1 serrano chili, steamed, seeded and finely diced*
⅓ cup tequila
2 tablespoons triple sec
¼ cup freshly squeezed lime juice
1 teaspoon cumin seeds, toasted and ground†
1 pound 16-20-count shrimp, peeled, deveined and
  butterflied
¼ cup olive oil
Kosher salt and freshly ground black pepper,
  to taste

SALAD

4 6-inch round corn tortillas
Vegetable oil, as needed for frying
1 teaspoon chili powder
1-2 tomatoes, seeded and diced**
1 yellow bell pepper, seeded and diced
6 cups torn romaine lettuce leaves, washed
  and patted dry

1. For the shrimp, in a large mixing bowl, combine the cilantro, garlic, chili, tequila, triple sec, lime juice and cumin. Add the shrimp and toss to coat. Allow the shrimp to marinate in the refrigerator for at least 1 hour.

2. Remove the shrimp from the marinade and set aside, reserving the marinade.

3. In a small saucepan over high heat, bring the marinade to a boil. Reduce the heat to medium and allow the marinade to simmer until it has reduced by half. Remove from the heat, transfer to a bowl and allow the marinade to cool.

4. Preheat a grill or broiler.

5. Once the marinade has cooled, whisk in the olive oil and season with salt and pepper, to taste. Set aside.

6. Grill or broil the shrimp until they are just pink (about 1 minute per side). Keep warm until service.

7. For the salad, fill a small skillet with vegetable oil to a depth of 1 inch. Place over medium heat. When the oil is about 375 degrees, fry the tortilla strips in batches in the hot oil until they are light brown and crisp. Drain on paper towels. While the strips are still warm, sprinkle them with chili powder.

8. In a large bowl, combine the tomato, bell pepper and lettuce. Add the marinade dressing and toss to coat. Top with the shrimp and fried tortilla strips and serve.

*To steam chili peppers, put into a Ziplock bag with 1 cup boiling water. Seal and hold for 5 minutes.

†To toast and grind cumin seeds, place them in a skillet over medium heat. Toast until they are fragrant, and then place the toasted seeds in the bowl of a spice or coffee grinder. Grind the seeds into a fine powder.

**Alternatively, Chef Demo recommends using canned Red Gold brand stewed tomatoes.

SERVES 4

FOLLOWING A FAMILY TRADITION

LIGHTER FARE

For Ivy Tech student Tracy Borel, her pursuit of a college degree is only sweetened by the specialty she chose. "I've always loved to cook. I would create little masterpieces with my Easy-Bake Oven, one of my favorite toys," she says.

An initial interest in radiology quickly gave way to the passion of Borel's youth and she switched her major to the culinary field. "One of my earliest influences was my great grandmother, Henriette Willis, 'Mama Red', who lived in Tennessee until she was 102. Everything we ate, she grew or raised. She taught me how to can produce and hand-turn vanilla ice cream."

With no permanent ties to Indianapolis, Borel has no qualms about traveling the globe in the name of culinary research. If she had to pick just one destination, the flavors of Chile have always enticed her palate. Back in the States, the Cajun/Creole dishes Borel grew up on are her specialty.

y Borel

JOEL RIFKIND, DDS
HOMETOWN: INDIANAPOLIS, INDIANA

AUTUMN HUES IN AN IMPRESSIVE VESSEL.

MUSHROOM-STUFFED ACORN SQUASH

BY JOEL RIFKIND, DDS
(PICTURED ON OPPOSITE PAGE)

Acorn squash hold up well through the winter as long as they are kept in a cool place. I like to be able to cook things from the garden in February when there are a couple of inches of snow on the ground. It is a reminder of how our ancestors would have sustained through the winters.

1 acorn squash
¼ cup unsalted butter, melted
¼ teaspoon garlic salt
1 pound button mushrooms, sliced
1 cup sour cream, to serve
Kosher salt and freshly ground black pepper,
  to taste

1. Preheat oven to 350 degrees.

2. Cut the acorn squash in half so that you have a top and a bottom. Remove the seeds.

3. Place the squash halves cut side down on a rimmed baking sheet. Pour water to ⅛-inch deep around the squash halves.

4. Bake in the 350-degree oven until tender (about 30 minutes).

5. Meanwhile, in a pan over medium heat, saute the mushrooms in the butter and garlic salt for about 3 minutes.

6. Remove the squash from the oven. To serve, place a squash half cut side up on a plate. Fill with the sauteed mushrooms and top with a dollop of sour cream. Season with salt and pepper, to taste.

SERVES 4

BAKED ACORN SQUASH
WITH CRANBERRY STUFFING

BY JOHNATHAN DEMO
(PICTURED BELOW, LEFT)

This is a perfect dish for Thanksgiving feasts. A true essence of everything fall.

4 small acorn squash
3 shallots, finely chopped
4 cloves garlic, crushed
2 tablespoons vegetable oil
1 red chili, seeds removed and finely chopped
1 tablespoon ground cumin
1 tablespoon ground coriander
1 tablespoon ground cinnamon
2 teaspoons ground ginger
1 cup minced pork
¼ cup pine nuts, toasted*
¼ cup dried cranberries
1 tablespoon chopped fresh parsley
Kosher salt and freshly ground black pepper,
  to taste
Steamed rice, to serve
Mixed leaves, to garnish

1. Preheat oven to 400 degrees.

2. Cut off the top of each squash and scoop out the seeds, reserving the tops. Cut a slice off the base of each squash so that the shell will stand upright on a baking sheet. Set aside.

3. In a skillet over medium heat, saute the shallots and the garlic in the vegetable oil until the shallots begin to brown. Add in the chili, cumin, coriander, cinnamon and ginger and continue to cook, stirring constantly, for 1 minute.

4. Stir in the pork and the nuts and cook until the pork has browned. Add the cranberries, parsley and salt and pepper, to taste. Remove from the heat.

5. Set the squash shells upright on an ungreased baking sheet. Into each shell, spoon enough of the pork mixture so that the shell is firmly packed. Replace the tops on the squash.

6. Bake on the middle rack of the 400-degree oven until the squash are soft and cooked through and the stuffing is piping hot (about 1 hour). Serve with the cooked rice and garnish with the mixed leaves.

SERVES 4

ASPARAGUS TOMATO QUICHE

BY RICK BRUNE
(PICTURED ON OPPOSITE PAGE, RIGHT)

This is a great early-summer breakfast or light entree for an afternoon lunch on the veranda.

4 eggs
3 tablespoons all-purpose flour
1 teaspoon kosher salt
1 teaspoon paprika
½ teaspoon dry mustard
1½ cups half-and-half
2 cups freshly grated Swiss cheese
1 10-inch pie shell, partially baked*
10 spears asparagus, trimmed and chopped into
  1-inch-long pieces
1 beefsteak tomato, sliced ¼-inch thick
Chopped fresh parsley, to garnish

RICK BRUNE
HOMETOWN: INDIANAPOLIS, INDIANA

A COLORFUL DISH TO IMPRESS.

1. Preheat oven to 375 degrees.

2. In a medium mixing bowl, beat the eggs with the flour, salt, paprika and mustard.

3. While still beating, slowly add in the half-and-half. Stir in the cheese and set aside.

4. Line the bottom of the pie shell with the asparagus pieces. Pour the egg mixture over the asparagus.

5. Bake in the 375-degree oven for 20 minutes.

6. Remove from the oven and top with tomato slices. Return the quiche to the oven and continue to bake for an additional 20-30 minutes.

7. Cut the quiche into 4 or 6 slices and place each slice on a warm plate. Garnish with fresh parsley and serve.

*To partially bake a pie shell, preheat oven to 375 degrees. Chill the pie shell in the refrigerator for 30 minutes. Line the bottom of the chilled pie shell with aluminum foil or parchment paper and top with pie weights or beans. Bake in the 375-degree oven for 15-20 minutes; remove the foil or paper and the pie weights and bake for an additional 5-10 minutes.

SERVES 4-6

ENJOY A SPICY PLAY ON TEXTURES.

CRUSTY BLACK BEAN ITALIAN SAUSAGE SUBS WITH ROASTED GREEN TOMATO SALSA

BY KIMBERLY KISER
(PICTURED ON OPPOSITE PAGE)

The roasted flavors from the tomatoes balance out much of the tartness from them. It has a great smoky-spicy flavor.

ROASTED GREEN TOMATO SALSA

2 tablespoons olive oil, plus more as needed
3 medium-sized green tomatoes, quartered
2 large cloves garlic, peeled
2 serrano peppers, chopped with ribs and seeds removed
½ cup fresh cilantro, coarsely chopped
¼ teaspoon freshy squeezed lime juice
Dash Worcestershire sauce
2 tablespoons-¼ cup water
½ Vidalia onion, finely chopped
Kosher salt, to taste

1. Preheat a broiler. Line a baking sheet with foil and coat it with olive oil.
2. In a medium bowl, toss the tomatoes and the garlic with 2 tablespoons olive oil until well coated. Spread the tomatoes and garlic on the prepared baking sheet.
3. Place the baking sheet in the oven until the tomatoes are well browned (about 15-20 minutes).
4. Put the tomatoes and garlic in a food processor or blender. Allow them to cool to room temperature.
5. Add the peppers, cilantro, lime juice, Worcestershire sauce and 2 tablespoons water. Process or blend until the mixture has the consistency of a coarse puree.
6. Pour the salsa into a bowl and thin with more water, if needed, until the consistency is "spoonable."
7. Stir in the onion and season with salt, to taste.

MAKES 1 ½-2 CUPS

SUBS

8 ounces Italian sausage, casings removed
3-4 tablespoons olive oil
2 15-ounce cans black beans, drained and rinsed or 3 ½ cups home-cooked black beans
Kosher salt, to taste
4 6-7-inch-long French rolls
16 slices pepper Jack cheese
1 ripe avocado, pitted, peeled and sliced ¼-inch thick
¾ cup Roasted Green Tomato Salsa

1. In a 12-inch skillet over medium heat, cook the sausage, using a spoon to break it up. Cook until sausage is browned and cooked through (about 8-9 minutes).
2. Stir in 1-2 tablespoons olive oil and the black beans. Bring the mixture to a simmer, and as it cooks, use a potato masher or the back of a spoon to mash the beans. Stir constantly and continue to cook until the beans are the consistency of very soft mashed potatoes. Season with salt, to taste.
3. Reduce the heat to low and cover the pan so that the beans remain warm but do not lose moisture and become hard.
4. Slice the French rolls in half and scoop out the soft bread from the center. Heat a large skillet or griddle over medium heat, add remaining olive oil and lay the roll halves on it cut side down. Cook until the rolls become crisp and golden brown.
5. Into the bottom half of each roll, smear about 1/2 cup of the hot sausage and bean mixture. Top with 4 slices of pepper Jack cheese and several slices of avocado.
6. Spoon on the roasted green tomato salsa, top with the other bread half and serve.

SERVES 4

DARCY SMINK
HOMETOWN: WEST LAFAYETTE, INDIANA

BOLD, ZESTY ITALIAN FLAVORS.

SMOKED GOUDA STROMBOLI

BY DARCY SMINK
(PICTURED ON OPPOSITE PAGE)

This Italian-style food is easy to pack for a picnic or lunch on the run. You can easily substitute out the filling ingredients to suit your own tastes

1 1-pound loaf frozen bread dough, thawed
½ cup marinara sauce, plus more to serve*
½ teaspoon dried Italian seasoning
6 ounces sliced pepperoni
2 cups shredded smoked Gouda cheese†
⅓ cup freshly grated Parmesan cheese

1. Preheat oven to 350 degrees. Grease a baking sheet.

2. On a floured work surface, punch down the thawed bread dough. Roll it out into a 20-by-8-inch rectangle, ½-inch thick. Place the rectangle onto the prepared baking sheet.

3. With the longer side of the rectangle facing you, spread the marinara sauce down the center third of the bread dough. Sprinkle the Italian seasoning on top of the sauce.

4. Layer the pepperoni slices on top of the seasoning, and then top with the shredded cheese.

5. Fold the left third of the dough over the filling, and then fold the right third of the dough over that. Pinch the ends together to seal. Sprinkle with the grated Parmesan.

6. Bake the stromboli in the 350-degree oven for 30 minutes, or until golden brown.

7. To serve, cut the stromboli into 6 pieces. Serve with additional marinara sauce.

*Use homemade marinara sauce or, for convenience, your favorite store-bought jarred sauce.

†Chef Smink recommends smoked Gouda from Fair Oaks Farms in Fair Oaks, Indiana, fofarms.com.

SERVES 6

PAUL ROBINSON'S CHICKEN ASPARAGUS
ENCHILADAS WITH CHIPOTLE HOLLANDAISE.

CAUSE FOR A FIESTA.

CHICKEN ASPARAGUS ENCHILADAS WITH CHIPOTLE HOLLANDAISE

BY PAUL ROBINSON
(PICTURED ON OPPOSITE PAGE)

The most wonderful chickens are at the local farmers markets; chickens that were raised running out in pastures and have more flavor. As Julia Child commented after having one, "[It's] really chicken-y."

ENCHILADAS

4 boneless, skinless chicken breasts
1 tablespoon olive oil
1 onion, diced
½ pint sour cream
1 cup shredded habanero Havarti cheese*
1 tablespoon dried parsley
½ teaspoon dried oregano
½ teaspoon freshly ground black pepper, plus more to taste
½ teaspoon kosher salt, plus more to taste
1 15-ounce jar salsa, plus more to serve†
½ cup chopped asparagus
1 clove garlic, minced
8 8-inch flour tortillas
2 tablespoons vegetable oil
2 tablespoons flour
1 tablespoon chili powder
Garlic powder, to taste
1 cup chicken broth
¾ cup shredded medium cheddar cheese*
Tortilla chips, to serve

CHIPOTLE HOLLANDAISE SAUCE

2 tablespoons vinegar
5 whole peppercorns
2 tablespoons water
2 egg yolks
1 tablespoon freshly squeezed lemon juice
1 cup clarified butter‡
Pinch ground cayenne pepper
1 7-ounce can chipotle peppers in adobo sauce, pureed

1. Preheat oven to 350 degrees.

2. In a skillet over medium-high heat, heat the olive oil. Add the chicken and cook until juices run clear (4-5 minutes per side). Drain, cool and cut into 1-inch cubes.

3. Return the chicken to the pan; add the onion, sour cream, Havarti, parsley, oregano and ½ teaspoon pepper. Cook over medium heat, stirring occasionally, until the cheese is melted.

4. Stir in ½ teaspoon salt, salsa, asparagus and garlic. Cook for 2 minutes, or until asparagus is slightly tender.

5. Divide the chicken mixture among the tortillas and roll them up to enclose the filling. Arrange them seam side down in a 9-by-13-inch baking dish. Set aside.

6. In a saucepan over medium heat, add the vegetable oil, flour, chili powder, pepper and garlic powder, to taste. Stir constantly; cook for 2 minutes until the mixture resembles a roux. Slowly whisk in the broth and allow to simmer until it is slightly thickened.

7. Top tortillas with sauce and sprinkle with cheddar cheese. Bake in the 350-degree oven for 20 minutes.

8. For the chipotle hollandaise sauce, put the vinegar and peppercorns in a saucepan and cook over medium heat until vinegar is reduced to a glaze. Stir in the water.

9. In the top of a double boiler over medium heat, whisk the egg yolks and vinegar until slightly thickened. Add in lemon juice and then gradually whisk in clarified butter, a little at a time, until fully incorporated. Season with salt and pepper, to taste. Remove from heat.

10. Stir in the pureed chipotle peppers and mix until they are well combined. Strain through a chinois.

11. Remove enchiladas from the oven and let rest for 10 minutes. Place 1 enchilada on each plate and top with hollandaise sauce. Serve with tortilla chips and salsa.

*Chef Robinson recommends using cheeses from Fair Oaks Farms in Fair Oaks, Indiana, fofarms.com.

†Chef Robinson prefers Crazy Charlie's brand salsa.

‡To make 1 cup clarified butter, in a saucepan over low heat, slowly melt 1¼ cups unsalted butter. As the butter melts, it will separate into three layers: a top foam layer, a clear golden-yellow middle layer (the clarified butter), and a bottom layer made up of milk solids. Using a spoon or ladle, skim off the top foamy layer and discard. Then, strain the butter through a fine sieve or cheesecloth to remove the milk solids. Clarified butter can be stored for 2-3 months in a refrigerator.

SERVES 8

AN OPTIMISTIC FOOD ADVENTURER

ENTRÉES

At just 26, Paul Robinson had concerns about his late start toward a culinary degree. But, he explains, "I have learned that there are plenty of people my age and older just getting started. Ivy Tech seems so much more diverse in that respect."

Robinson, from Lafayette, Indiana, can trace the roots of his culinary interests back through his family tree. "My grandmother was always making pies from scratch and homemade chicken 'n noodles. And my grandfather, while not a cook, was constantly tending his garden." It was these images perhaps that have led Robinson to work in quick-service restaurants for the past 10 years and challenge himself further at Ivy Tech Community College. With an interest in the dishes of Latin America, Robinson would love the opportunity to go "beyond Indiana's cornfields."

Robinson has several dishes featured in this book, including Grilled Walleye with Sweet Corn and Black Bean Relish (page 47). With hopes to graduate in 2011, this young chef in the making credits the team of inspirational instructors at Ivy Tech for making him feel as though the sky is the limit.

PAUL ROBINSON
HOMETOWN: LAFAYETTE INDIANA

A FRESH TAKE ON THE CATCH OF THE DAY.

LAKE PERCH POACHED IN OLIVER'S BEANBLOSSOM BLUSH
WITH INDIANA MUSKMELON CHUTNEY

BY PAUL ROBINSON
(PICTURED ON THE OPPOSITE PAGE)

I GREW UP IN A LAKE COMMUNITY in northern Indiana. I remember sitting on the end of a pier on those hot afternoons with a fishing pole trailing into the water. We would pull in one perch after another. This recipe captures the essence of late summer in Indiana.

CHUTNEY

4 cups large-dice Indiana muskmelon
½ cup medium-dice yellow onion
¾ cup apple cider vinegar
¾ cup brown sugar
1 tablespoon minced ginger
⅛ teaspoon kosher salt
⅓ cup raisins

LAKE PERCH

4 cups Oliver's Beanblossom Blush wine
2 sprigs fresh rosemary
1 lemon, sliced
Kosher salt and pepper, to taste
4 6-ounce perch filets
Fresh mint leaves, to garnish
1 lemon, cut into wedges, to garnish

1. For the chutney, in a saucepan, combine all of the ingredients. Bring the mixture to a boil, then reduce the heat. Allow the chutney to simmer for 30-35 minutes, stirring frequently.

2. Remove from heat, cool and chill in the refrigerator until service.

3. For the lake perch, in a saucepan, combine the wine, rosemary, lemon slices and salt and pepper, to taste. Bring the mixture to a boil and then reduce the heat to a slow simmer.

4. Add the fish filets and continue to simmer until they are cooked through (about 6-7 minutes).

5. To serve, place 1 filet on each plate. Garnish with fresh mint leaves and a lemon wedge and serve with the muskmelon chutney.

SERVES 4

BASIL BLOOD ORANGE WHITEFISH FILETS BY STUDENT DARCY SMINK. RECIPE ON PAGE 46.

BASIL BLOOD ORANGE-WHITEFISH FILETS

BY DARCY SMINK
(PICTURED ON PAGE 45)

BLOOD ORANGES ARE A RARE AND WONDERFUL THING. True blood (moro) oranges are only produced when there is a freeze in California or Florida near the end of citrus growing season (January/February). The freeze produces the dark red color in the juice.

1 cup firmly packed fresh basil leaves
Juice of 6 blood oranges
2 tablespoons freshly squeezed lemon juice
4 tablespoons olive oil
4 teaspoons orange zest
4 8-ounce whitefish filets
Steamed wild rice, to serve
Steamed asparagus, to serve

1. Thinly slice the fresh basil leaves.
2. In a stainless steel bowl, whisk together the basil, blood orange juice, lemon juice, olive oil and the orange zest to make a marinade.
3. Place the whitefish filets in a 2-gallon zip-top plastic bag. Pour the marinade over the fish and tightly seal the bag, removing as much air as possible. Allow the fish to marinate in the refrigerator for 30-60 minutes.
4. Preheat oven to 350 degrees.
5. Remove the fish from the marinade and place the filets on a rimmed baking sheet. Discard the marinade.
6. Bake the fish in the 350-degree oven until it easily flakes when a fork is inserted (about 6-10 minutes per inch of thickness). The fish should be opaque in color and slightly firm to the touch.
7. To serve, plate the fish alongside a serving of wild rice and steamed asparagus.

SERVES 4

WHITEFISH VERACRUZ

BY BONNIE WILSON
(PICTURED BELOW, RIGHT)

IN THIS RECIPE, BONNIE CONVERTS A CLASSIC MEXICAN DISH using a local fish species. The finished entree is spicy without being overpowering.

6 4-ounce fresh or frozen whitefish filets
$\frac{1}{8}$ teaspoon kosher salt
$\frac{1}{8}$ teaspoon freshly ground black pepper
1 tablespoon olive oil
1 large onion, sliced and separated into rings
2 cloves garlic, minced
2 large tomatoes, chopped
$\frac{1}{4}$ cup sliced pimento-stuffed olives
$\frac{1}{4}$ cup dry white wine
2 tablespoons capers, drained
1-2 jalapeño or serrano peppers, stems and seeds removed, and chopped
$\frac{1}{2}$ teaspoon sugar
1 bay leaf

1. Thaw the fish if it is frozen. Rinse and pat dry, and season with the salt and black pepper.
2. In a large skillet over medium heat, heat the oil. Add the onion and garlic and cook until the onion becomes tender.
3. Stir in the tomatoes, olives, wine, capers, jalapeño or serrano peppers, sugar and bay leaf. Bring the mixture to a boil and add the fish. Reduce the heat, cover and simmer until the fish easily flakes when a fork is inserted (about 6-10 minutes).
4. Using a slotted spoon, carefully transfer the fish from the skillet to a serving platter. Cover the fish and keep warm until service.
5. Return the sauce in the skillet to a boil. Stirring occasionally, allow it to cook until it has reduced to about 2 cups (about 5-6 minutes). Discard the bay leaf.
6. Spoon the sauce over the fish and serve.

SERVES 6

GRILLED WALLEYE
WITH SWEET CORN AND BLACK BEAN RELISH

BY PAUL ROBINSON
(PICTURED BELOW, LEFT)

THE GREAT INDIANA OUTDOORS MEET THE SOUTHWEST with this refreshing well-seasoned blend of flavors.

GRILLED WALLEYE

⅓ cup cider vinegar
2 tablespoons extra-virgin olive oil,
 plus more as needed
2 tablespoons finely chopped fresh cilantro,
 plus more to garnish
1 clove garlic, minced
1 teaspoon ground cumin
1 jalapeño, minced and seeds removed
4 6-ounce walleye filets

SWEET CORN AND BLACK BEAN RELISH

⅔ cup canned black beans, drained and rinsed*
¼ cup Indiana sweet corn
¼ cup small-dice yellow bell pepper
¼ cup small-dice red bell pepper
¼ cup small-dice green bell pepper
¼ cup small-dice red onion
1 tablespoon Worcestershire sauce
¼ teaspoon ground cumin
⅛ teaspoon ground cayenne pepper
Kosher salt and freshly ground black pepper,
 to taste

1. For the grilled walleye, in a medium bowl, combine the vinegar, 2 tablespoons olive oil, cilantro, garlic, ground cumin and jalapeño. Add the fish filets. Chill in the refrigerator for 1 hour, turning the fish at least once while it is marinating.

2. Meanwhile, for the sweet corn and black bean relish, in a medium bowl, combine all the ingredients (black beans, corn, bell peppers, onions, Worcestershire sauce, cumin, cayenne pepper and salt and pepper, to taste). Chill in the refrigerator for 1 hour.

3. Preheat a grill to hot and brush the cooking grates with oil.

4. Remove the filets from the marinade and discard the marinade. Grill the filets on the preheated grill until cooked through (about 3-5 minutes per side).

5. Remove the sweet corn and black bean relish from the refrigerator and adjust seasoning, if necessary, with salt and pepper, to taste.

6. To serve, divide the chilled relish among four plates. Top with the fish and garnish with the chopped cilantro, to taste.

Chef Robinson recommends using Hurst's brand canned black beans.

SERVES 4

PAUL ROBINSON
HOMETOWN: LAFAYETTE, INDIANA

FISH AND CHIPS FROM THE HEARTLAND.

SMOKED CATFISH WITH HOME FRIES AND PERSIMMON KETCHUP

BY PAUL ROBINSON
(PICTURED ON OPPOSITE PAGE)

I LIKE WHAT PAUL HAS DONE HERE. He uses Indiana staples and creates a full meal. I could see this being served as breakfast in New Orleans or a soul food dinner.

SMOKED CATFISH

2 cups water
1 cup freshly squeezed lemon juice
5 cloves garlic, sliced
4 shallots, sliced
2 tablespoons salt
2 tablespoons sugar
6 8-ounce catfish filets
Vegetable oil, as needed

PERSIMMON KETCHUP

1 quart pitted and small-dice persimmons
$1/4$ cup white wine vinegar
1 small stick cinnamon
$1/4$ teaspoon black peppercorns
2 teaspoons lemon zest

HOME FRIES

3-4 pounds Idaho potatoes cut into large julienne
Vegetable oil, as needed

1. For the smoked catfish, in a medium bowl, combine the water, lemon juice, garlic, shallots, salt and sugar to make a marinade.

2. Place the catfish filets in a shallow baking dish. Pour the marinade over the fish and cover with plastic wrap. Marinate in the refrigerator for 4-5 hours.

3. Preheat a grill to 250 degrees or let the coals burn down to medium-to-low heat. Oil the grill racks.

4. Cook the fish on the grill until it easily flakes when a fork is inserted (about 25 minutes).

5. Meanwhile, for the persimmon ketchup, in a saucepan over low heat, combine the persimmons, vinegar, cinnamon stick, peppercorns and lemon zest. Allow the mixture to simmer until the liquid evaporates (about 30 minutes). Remove the cinnamon stick and peppercorns.

6. For the home fries, in a deep, heavy-bottomed pan, place vegetable oil to a depth of 5 inches. Heat the oil over high heat. When the oil is hot, fry the potatoes in batches until tender (about 5 minutes). Drain on paper towel-lined plates and keep warm for service.

7. Divide the home fries among 6 plates. Place a catfish filet on each and serve with persimmon ketchup.

SERVES 6

BONNIE WILSON
HOMETOWN: INDIANAPOLIS, INDIANA

A GULF COAST–MIDWEST HYBRID.

BISCUIT-TOPPED CHICKEN GUMBO PIE

BY BONNIE WILSON
(PICTURED ON OPPOSITE PAGE)

THIS IS A GUMBO-MEETS-POT-PIE SCENARIO.
Comfort food of the Gulf Coast intersects with comfort
food of the Midwest.

CHICKEN GUMBO

3 tablespoons plus 1 teaspoon vegetable oil
3 tablespoons all-purpose flour
3 tablespoons unsalted butter
¾ pound smoked sausage, sliced ¼-inch thick
4 boneless, skinless chicken breasts, julienned
1 large onion, chopped
2 cloves garlic, minced
½ green bell pepper, chopped
½ red bell pepper, chopped
1 small rib celery, minced
3 tablespoons rice, uncooked
2 cups chicken stock
2 teaspoons freshly squeezed lemon juice
¼ pound okra, sliced
½ cup fresh or frozen, thawed corn
2 tablespoons ground cayenne pepper
Kosher salt and freshly ground black pepper,
  to taste

BISCUIT TOPPING

2 cups flour
1 tablespoon baking powder
2 teaspoons sugar
½ teaspoon kosher salt
6½ tablespoons unsalted butter, cold
¾ cup buttermilk

1. For the chicken gumbo, in a heavy-bottomed skillet, combine 3 tablespoons vegetable oil with the flour to make a roux. Cook over low heat, stirring occasionally, until the mixture is dark mahogany in color (about 1 hour). Remove from the heat and set aside.

2. In a medium casserole pan or Dutch oven over medium heat, melt 2 tablespoons butter with the remaining 1 teaspoon vegetable oil. Add the sausage and cook until well browned (about 5 minutes). Transfer the sausage to a plate.

3. To the pan, add the chicken. Cook over medium heat until lightly browned (about 7 minutes). Transfer the chicken to a separate plate.

4. To the pan, add the remaining 1 tablespoon butter and the onion. Cook over medium heat until the onion is softened and translucent (about 2 minutes). Reduce the heat to low and add the garlic, green and red bell peppers, celery and rice. Cook, stirring constantly, for an additional 5 minutes.

5. Stir the roux into the casserole pan with the vegetables and rice. Add in the chicken stock and lemon juice, and bring the mixture to a boil.

6. Stir in the sausage and chicken. Reduce the heat to low and cook, covered, for 25 minutes. Stir in the okra, corn and cayenne pepper and season with salt and pepper, to taste. Continue to cook for an additional 2 minutes, stirring occasionally, and then remove from the heat.

7. Preheat oven to 450 degrees.

8. For the biscuit topping, in a medium bowl, combine the flour and baking powder. Cut in 5½ tablespoons cold butter until the mixture is coarse and crumbly. Stir in the buttermilk until a dough forms.

9. On a lightly floured work surface, roll out the dough to a ½-inch thickness. Cut out 12 round biscuits.

10. Pour the gumbo into a shallow 9-inch round baking dish. Arrange the biscuits on top and brush with the melted butter (the remaining 1 tablespoon). Bake in the 450-degree oven until the biscuits are puffed up and golden brown (about 30 minutes).

11. Divide the gumbo pie equally among 6 warm bowls and serve.

SERVES 6

MAPLE LEAF DUCK ETOUFFEE
WITH WILD RICE

BY PAUL ROBINSON
(PICTURED AT RIGHT)

MAPLE LEAF FARMS IS THE LARGEST PRODUCER OF DUCK IN THE UNITED STATES, yet Indiana is one of the lowest consumers of duck in the country. People often tell me they find duck too oily. In truth, when prepared correctly, duck is much leaner than chicken or even pork. The natural oils must be seared out of the fat before final cooking. Or, in the case of this recipe, the skin can be removed altogether.

6 tablespoons unsalted butter
3 tablespoons all-purpose flour
1 cup medium-dice yellow onions
6 green onions, thinly sliced
½ cup diced green bell peppers
½ cup diced celery
2 cups chicken stock
3 cups wild rice
3 pounds boneless, skinless duck breasts, thinly sliced*
¼ cup chopped fresh parsley
Kosher salt and freshly ground black pepper, to taste
1 bay leaf
Mild to Wild Pepper and Herb Co. Red Savina Garlic Hot Sauce, to taste
1 loaf crusty French bread, sliced, to serve

1. In a saucepan over low heat, melt the butter. Whisk in the flour to make a roux. Stir constantly until the mixture is golden brown and has a nutty aroma, about 10 minutes.

2. Stir in the yellow and green onions, green pepper and celery. Raise the heat to medium and cook until the onions are translucent, about 7 minutes.

3. Add in the stock, rice, duck meat, parsley and bay leaf. Bring the mixture to a simmer and cook until the rice is tender, about 20 minutes.

4. Season with salt, pepper and hot sauce, to taste. Ladle into bowls and serve with crusty French bread.

*Chef Robinson recommends using duck from Maple Leaf Farms in Milford, Indiana, mapleleaffarms.com.

SERVES 10

MOJO ROASTED PORK

BY RICK BRUNE
(PICTURED BELOW)

IT'S THE MOJO BABY! Rick twists this classic Mexican dish into a Midwestern favorite.

CUBAN MOJO MARINADE

1 cup freshly squeezed orange juice
½ cup freshly squeezed lime juice
5 ounces ¼-inch-dice yellow onion
2 tablespoons minced garlic
½ teaspoon ground cumin
1 tablespoon chopped fresh Indiana-grown oregano
½ teaspoon freshly ground black pepper
1 teaspoon kosher salt
3 tablespoons chopped fresh cilantro
1 cup olive oil
1 4-5-pound pork tenderloin

MOJO SAUCE

½ cup vegetable broth
½ cup freshly squeezed lime juice
1 cup freshly squeezed orange juice
1 cup ¼-inch-dice yellow onions
1 cup ¼-inch-dice Indiana plum tomatoes
½ cup ¼-inch-dice red bell pepper
¼ cup ¼-inch-dice green onions
1 tablespoon chopped fresh Indiana-grown oregano
2 tablespoons chopped fresh cilantro
1 tablespoon minced garlic
½ teaspoon ground allspice
¼ teaspoon ground cinnamon
¾ teaspoon freshly ground black pepper
½ teaspoon dried thyme
Pinch ground cayenne pepper

1. For the Cuban mojo marinade, in a large bowl, combine all of the ingredients except for the pork (orange juice, lime juice, onion, garlic, cumin, oregano, pepper, salt, cilantro and olive oil).

2. Pour the marinade over the pork tenderloin, turning to evenly coat the meat. Allow the pork to marinate overnight in the refrigerator.

3. Preheat a grill to 350 degrees or preheat an oven to 375 degrees.

4. For the mojo sauce, in the bowl of a food processor, combine all of the ingredients (broth, lime juice, orange juice, yellow onions, tomatoes, bell pepper, green onions, oregano, cilantro, garlic, allspice, cinnamon, pepper, thyme and cayenne pepper). Process until the mixture is smooth.

5. Transfer the sauce to a saucepan and bring it to a boil. Reduce the heat and cook for 2-3 minutes, stirring frequently. Keep hot until service.

6. Remove pork tenderloin from the marinade and drain. Grill the pork on the 350-degree grill until an internal temperature of 155 degrees is achieved (about 5-7 minutes per side). Or, alternatively, roast the tenderloin in the 375-degree oven for about 35 minutes.

7. To serve, slice the pork tenderloin and plate it. Top with a generous ladle of the mojo sauce.

SERVES 4

DARCY SMINK
HOMETOWN: WEST LAFAYETTE, INDIANA

THE CARIBBEAN, FLORIDA AND INDIANA.

FLORIBBEAN PORK TENDERLOIN MEDALLIONS

BY DARCY SMINK
(PICTURED ON OPPOSITE PAGE)

FLORIBBEAN IS A GRAND BLENDING OF CUISINES from the Caribbean and Florida. It is a real melting pot of fruits, spices from the spice trade days, French cooking techniques and seasonal ingredients.

1 1-pound pork tenderloin*
¼ cup Madras curry powder
1 cup all-purpose flour, sifted
8 tablespoons unsalted butter
1 cup diced papaya
½ cup cream of coconut†
2 bananas, peeled and sliced ½-inch thick
½ cup dark rum
½ cup unsweetened coconut flakes, toasted**

1. Pat dry the pork tenderloin and slice crosswise into 1-inch rounds.

2. In a shallow pan or bowl, combine the curry powder and the flour. Mix well.

3. Dredge the pork medallions in the curry-flour mixture, being careful to shake off any excess. Set aside.

4. In a large saute pan over medium-high heat, melt 4 tablespoons butter. Add the pork medallions and cook until the medallions are brown on both sides, but still moist and slightly pink in the center (about 2 minutes per side).

5. Drain any excess butter from the pan. Leave the medallions in the pan. Return the pan to the heat and add the cream of coconut, papaya and bananas. Stir to combine.

6. Carefully pour in the rum and flambé until the alcohol burns off.

7. Add the remaining 4 tablespoons butter to the pan. Stir until melted and heated through.

8. To serve, place 3 medallions on the center of each plate. Top with the coconut sauce, being careful to include bananas and papaya on each plate. Garnish with 2 tablespoons of the toasted coconut flakes.

*Chef Smink recommends using pork tenderloin from Royer Farm in Clinton, Indiana, royerfarmfresh.com.

†You may be tempted to use coconut milk, but don't. Though similar to coconut milk, cream of coconut contains less water. Find it in a liquor store or in the drinks/mixers section of a well-stocked grocery store.

**To toast coconut, preheat oven to 350 degrees. Spread the shredded coconut flakes on a rimmed baking sheet and bake in the 350-degree oven for 5-10 minutes or until golden, stirring once or twice to prevent the coconut from browning unevenly.

SERVES 4

DARCY SMINK
HOMETOWN: WEST LAFAYETTE. INDIANA

SWEETEN THIS UNDERAPPRECIATED MEAT.

MEDALLIONS OF VENISON
WITH BLUEBERRY CHUTNEY

BY DARCY SMINK
(PICTURED ON OPPOSITE PAGE)

MANY PEOPLE ARE APPREHENSIVE ABOUT COOK-
ING VENISON. It is actually a wonderful meat to cook
with that marries very well with fruits.

VENISON MEDALLIONS

1 cup buttermilk
½ cup raspberry vinegar
3 bay leaves
8 3-3½-ounce medallions venison*
Kosher salt and freshly ground black pepper,
  to taste
3 tablespoons unsalted butter

BLUEBERRY CHUTNEY

1 small red onion, chopped
1 clove garlic, chopped
1 lime, sliced into thin wedges
¼ cup crystallized ginger
1 jalapeño, diced and seeds removed
1 cup raspberry vinegar
2 pounds fresh blueberries†
1 cup firmly packed dark brown sugar
1 teaspoon kosher salt
1 teaspoon ground cinnamon
½ teaspoon ground allspice
½ teaspoon ground cloves
½ cup golden raisins

1. For the venison medallions, in a small bowl, combine
the buttermilk, raspberry vinegar and bay leaves.

2. Season the venison medallions on both sides with
salt and pepper, to taste. Place them in a 2-gallon zip-
top bag and pour the buttermilk mixture over the meat.
Seal the bag tightly, removing as much air as possible.
Allow the venison to marinate for 1 hour at room
temperature or up to 24 hours in the refrigerator.

3. Remove the venison from the marinade and pat
dry. Discard the marinade.

4. In a large saute pan over medium-high heat, melt
the butter. Working in batches, saute the medallions
until they are medium-rare (about 2 minutes per side).
Be careful not to overcook the meat. Remove from the
pan and keep warm until service.

5. For the blueberry chutney, in the bowl of a food
processor, combine the onion, garlic, lime, ginger and
jalapeño. Process until finely chopped and combined.
Add ½ cup raspberry vinegar and puree until smooth.

6. Place the blueberries in a large saucepan. Stir in
the pureed onion mixture, brown sugar, salt, cinnamon,
allspice, cloves and the remaining ½ cup raspberry
vinegar. Bring the mixture to a boil and then reduce
the heat to medium. Simmer uncovered, stirring
occasionally, until thickened (about 45 minutes).

7. During the last 15 minutes of cooking, add the
golden raisins to the pan.

8. To serve, place 2 venison medallions in the center
of each plate. Top with ½ cup blueberry chutney.**

*Chef Smink recommends using venison meat from
Double T Ranch in Martinsville, Indiana, 888.349.1889.*

†*Chef Smink recommends acquiring blueberries from
Prelock Blueberry Farm in Lafayette, Indiana,
prelockblueberryfarm.com.*

**Chef Smink suggests braised cabbage and baked po-
tatoes would be a tasty accompaniment to this dish.*

SERVES 4

JOHNATHAN DEMO
HOMETOWN: FLINT, MICHIGAN

GET SPICY WITH A MIDWEST STANDARD.

TWISTED POT ROAST (SOUTHWEST STYLE)

BY JOHNATHAN DEMO
(PICTURED ON OPPOSITE PAGE)

POT ROAST IS A TRUE COMFORT FOOD. This play on the classic will warm you up.

1½ cups white wine
3 tablespoons white wine vinegar
4 mild green chilies, steamed, peeled and chopped
3 tablespoons brown sugar
1 tablespoon kosher salt
3 cloves garlic, finely minced
3 pounds beef round steak
1 strip bacon
2-3 tablespoons unsalted butter
1 large onion, sliced
¾ cup beef stock
3-4 tablespoons tomato paste

1. In a medium bowl, combine the wine, vinegar, chilies, brown sugar, salt and garlic to make a marinade.

2. Place the meat in a shallow, flat-bottom pan just large enough to hold it, and pour the marinade over it. Turn the beef to evenly coat it with the marinade. Cover and chill in the refrigerator overnight, checking 2-3 times to turn and baste the meat with the marinade.

3. Remove the beef from the marinade, reserving the marinade.

4. In a small skillet over medium-high heat, cook the bacon until it is crispy. Remove it from the heat and allow it to cool, reserving the fat in the pan. Once it is cooled, mince the bacon.

5. In a large Dutch oven, melt the butter. Add the beef and cook until it is thoroughly browned on all sides.

6. Stir in 1½ cups of the reserved marinade, along with the onion, minced bacon and reserved bacon fat, beef stock and tomato paste. Bring the mixture to a boil. Cover the pan and allow the mixture to simmer for 45 minutes.

7. Preheat oven to 325 degrees.

8. Transfer the Dutch oven from the stovetop to the oven. Bake in the 325-degree oven until the beef is tender (about 1½ hours).

9. Remove the beef from the pan, reserving the liquid in the pan. Allow the beef to rest on the countertop.

10. Transfer the pan liquid to a saucepan. Bring the mixture to a simmer over high heat and allow it to reduce for 5 minutes.

11. Slice the beef and plate it. Spoon the sauce over top and serve.

SERVES 6-8

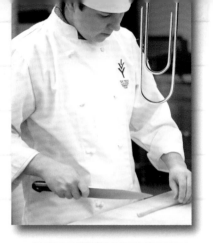

FROM THE SEAS TO SARAH'S GARDEN

SIDE DISHES

As a veteran of the United States Coast Guard and recipient of the Montgomery GI Bill, Sarah Nunery appreciates the opportunity to pursue her dream at an appealing price tag. "I have wanted to be a chef my entire life," she says. "My parents love food and have an appreciation for staying healthy through the options they cook for the family. Since the tuition at Ivy Tech is so affordable, I can go to school full time and just focus on the work."

The 32-year-old Campbellsville, Kentucky, native drew from the culinary influences of the South for her recipe, Fresh Fried Okra from Sarah's Garden (page 65). Along with her general culinary degree, she plans to pursue a baking degree as well. Nunery found additional inspiration from the instructors and the curriculum at the college. "The chefs are talented and patient, and always there if you need help. This program really forces us to dig deeper and further our education." Nunery doesn't' rule out traveling to expand her culinary knowledge when she graduates in 2011, but considers Indiana her new permanent home.

BONNIE WILSON
HOMETOWN: INDIANAPOLIS. INDIANA

FRESH FROM THE FARMERS MARKET.

ZUCCHINI
MUSHROOM
CASSEROLE

BY BONNIE WILSON
(PICTURED AT RIGHT)

There is a time when everyone with a garden is trying to give away zucchini. It is a prolific plant, and this recipe is a great way to use it.

½ cup olive oil
½ cup julienned onion
2 ounces mushrooms, sliced
½ teaspoon kosher salt
¼ teaspoon freshly ground black pepper
1 cup bread crumbs
3 eggs
3 large zucchini, sliced ¼-inch thick
1 10-ounce can cream of mushroom soup
¼ cup milk
1 teaspoon dried rosemary
8 ounces shredded cheddar cheese
½ cup freshly grated Parmesan cheese
Fresh rosemary sprigs, to garnish

1. Preheat oven to 350 degrees. Grease an 8-by-8-inch baking dish.

2. In a skillet over medium-high heat, heat the olive oil. Add the onions and mushrooms and saute for 1 minute, or until the onions are light brown. Remove from heat and set aside.

3. On a sheet of waxed paper, mix together the salt, pepper and bread crumbs.

4. In a shallow bowl, lightly beat the eggs.

5. Dip the zucchini slices in the bread crumbs, then the eggs and then again in the bread crumbs. In a separate pan, add oil and fry the zucchini slices in batches until they are golden brown (about 5 minutes per side).

6. In a large bowl, combine soup, milk and rosemary.

7. Pour half of the soup mixture into the prepared baking dish. Top with half of the zucchini and then half of the mushrooms, followed by half of the cheddar and then half of the Parmesan. Repeat the layers (soup, zucchini and mushrooms, cheddar, Parmesan).

8. Bake uncovered in the 350-degree oven until hot and bubbly (about 30 minutes). Serve, garnished with fresh rosemary sprigs.

SERVES 6

MIRLITON
WITH SAUTEED
CORN STUFFING*

BY DARCY SMINK
(PICTURED ON OPPOSITE PAGE)

Mirliton, part of the squash family, is also called chayote, Buddha's hands and praying hands. The type we usually see is green, similar in shape to a pear and, as long as it's cooked, the flesh and skin can both be consumed. The photograph of this dish shows an Asian mirliton, which is harder to come by and does not offer an edible casing.

3 mirlitons (chayote squash), halved and seeded
3 ears sweet Indiana corn, husked and cleaned
2 tablespoons olive oil
3 scallions, both white and green parts, chopped
½ cup finely diced red bell pepper
½ cup chopped fresh Italian parsley
½ cup finely diced boiled ham
1 teaspoon minced fresh thyme
Kosher salt and freshly ground black pepper, to taste
Ground cayenne pepper, to taste
½ cup fresh bread crumbs

1. Bring a stockpot of salted water to a boil. Cook the mirliton halves until tender, but still firm (6-10 minutes).

2. Remove mirliton from the pot and set upside down to cool. When cool enough to handle, scoop out the inside pulp, leaving a shell about ⅓-inch thick. Reserve the pulp and place the shells in a small baking dish.

3. Chop the mirliton pulp and set aside. Preheat oven to 375 degrees.

4. Cut the kernels from the ears of corn.

5. In a pan over medium-high heat, heat the olive oil. Add the corn kernels and saute for 2 minutes. Remove the corn from the pan and set aside.

6. Add the chopped mirliton pulp to the pan, along with the scallions, bell pepper, parsley, ham, thyme, corn, and salt, pepper and cayenne pepper, to taste. Cook over medium-high heat until all of the liquid has evaporated (about 4 minutes). Stir in the corn kernels.

7. Divide the filling among the 6 mirliton shells. Top with bread crumbs.

8. Bake in the 375-degree oven until browned and heated through (about 35 minutes). Remove from the oven and serve immediately.

Chef Smink suggests pairing this dish with a main pork entree.

SERVES 6

SARAH NUNERY
HOMETOWN: CAMPBELLSVILLE, KENTUCKY

A SOUTHERN FAVORITE FRIED GOLDEN BROWN.

FRESH FRIED OKRA
FROM SARAH'S GARDEN

BY SARAH NUNERY
(PICTURED ON OPPOSITE PAGE)

Okra grows well in Indiana. The fried okra would be great with the persimmon ketchup included with the smoked catfish recipe (page 49).

14 ounces okra, cut into ½-inch rings
Kosher salt and freshly ground black pepper,
  to taste
½ cup all-purpose flour
½ cup milk
2 eggs, lightly beaten
⅔ cup fresh bread crumbs
½ cup cooking oil*

1. Season the okra with salt and pepper, to taste, and let it sit for 2-3 minutes.

2. Meanwhile, in 4 separate shallow dishes, place the flour, milk, eggs and bread crumbs.

3. Dip the okra slices first in the milk, then in the flour, then in the eggs, and lastly in the bread crumbs.

4. In a skillet over medium heat, heat the oil. Working in batches, fry the coated okra slices in the hot oil for 4 minutes on each side.

5. Drain and season with salt and pepper, to taste. Serve immediately.

*If available, Chef Nunery suggests frying the okra in bacon fat.

SERVES 6

SOUTHERN COLLARDS

BY JOHNATHAN DEMO
(PICTURED BELOW)

This recipe is for a classic of the South, as well as the Midwestern farm table. Enjoy with catfish for a true Southern experience.

3 large bunches (about 2 pounds) collard greens
3 tablespoons olive oil
6 large scallions, both white and green parts,
  trimmed and thinly sliced
3 large cloves garlic, finely chopped
¼ teaspoon freshly ground black pepper
Kosher salt, to taste

1. Remove the coarse central veins from the collard greens. Stack 4-5 leaves together and slice at 1-inch intervals. Continue until all the greens are sliced.

2. Wash the greens well in several changes of cool water. Spin the collards in a salad spinner and then pat dry on a paper towel. Set aside.

3. In a large, deep skillet over medium-high heat, heat the olive oil for 2 minutes. Add the scallions and garlic and stir-fry until they are limp and golden (about 5 minutes).

4. Add the collards and pepper and stir-fry until the leaves glisten and begin to wilt (about 5 minutes). Cover and steam until the greens are crisp-tender (about 10-15 minutes).

5. Remove from the pan and season with salt, to taste. Serve alongside chicken, pork or baked ham.

SERVES 4-6

JOHNATHAN DEMO
HOMETOWN: FLINT, MICHIGAN

VIBRANTLY COLORED WITH THE FLAVORS TO MATCH.

FRIED GREEN TOMATOES WITH GREEN CHILIES AND CREAM

BY JOHNATHAN DEMO
(PICTURED ON OPPOSITE PAGE)

This is a great recipe to use some of the green tomatoes that are left after the first frost. I also like to grow green zebra tomatoes and fry them when they are fully ripe to have a much fruitier taste.

¾ cup finely ground blue cornmeal
1 teaspoon kosher salt
2 teaspoons minced fresh basil
4 green tomatoes, sliced 1-inch thick
¼ cup unsalted butter
4 green chilies, poached, peeled and chopped
1½ cups sour cream

1. In a shallow bowl, combine the blue cornmeal, salt and basil.

2. Dip each tomato slice in the cornmeal mixture, gently pressing down to make sure that the cornmeal sticks.

3. In a skillet over medium-high heat, melt the butter. Add the tomato slices and brown on both sides.

4. Spread the green chilies evenly over the tops of the tomato slices. Cover and allow the tomatoes to steam for about 5 minutes, or until the chilies are heated through. Remove the tomatoes and green chilies from the skillet.

5. To the hot skillet, add the sour cream. Allow the cream to simmer over medium-high heat for 5 minutes.

6. To serve, place the fried tomatoes on a plate and top with the hot sour cream.

SERVES 4-6

INDIANA AUGUST SALSA

BY JENNIFER K. HALLBERG
(PICTURED BELOW)

This fruit salsa is a great dessert for a late summer dinner party.

3 ounces cantaloupe, peeled and medium-dice
2 ounces seedless red grapes, halved
2 ounces peaches, pitted, peeled and medium-dice
1 tablespoon freshly squeezed lime juice
½ tablespoon chopped fresh cilantro
½ tablespoon chopped fresh mint leaves

1. In a medium bowl, combine all the ingredients. Cover and refrigerate overnight.

2. Serve chilled alongside grilled chicken or fish.

MAKES 2 CUPS

JOEL RIFKIND, DDS
HOMETOWN: INDIANAPOLIS, INDIANA

A DISH WORTHY OF THE STATE FAIR.

POPCORN-CRUSTED ONION RINGS

BY JOEL RIFKIND, DDS
(PICTURED ON OPPOSITE PAGE)

Indiana is the leading popcorn producer. Personally, my favorite varietal is Lady Finger; the smaller hulls make for a brighter popcorn flavor.

Vegetable oil, for deep frying
1 large sweet onion, sliced 1/4-inch thick
2/3 cup water
2/3 cup all-purpose flour
Popped popcorn, as needed, white parts separated
  from the hulls and finely chopped
1 teaspoon garlic powder, or to taste
1 teaspoon kosher salt, or to taste

1. Separate the onion slices into rings.

2. In a shallow bowl, whisk together the water and flour until smooth. In a separate shallow bowl, place the chopped popcorn.

3. Line a baking pan with paper towels. To a deep heavy-bottomed pan, add oil to a depth of 5 inches. Heat the oil to 375 degrees.

4. Dip the onion rings in the flour mix. Shake slightly to remove any excess, then dip in popcorn, being sure to coat the onions evenly.

5. Fry the rings until they are golden brown (1-2 minutes). Drain on the paper towel-lined baking pan. Continue until all of them are cooked.

6. Sprinkle the onions with garlic powder and salt, to taste, and serve immediately.

SERVES 4

JALAPENO CHEDDAR CORNBREAD

BY JAMIE MARKS
(PICTURED BELOW)

At the State Fair each year they grind different flours and corn. I like to go and stock up because the fresh ground grains are more flavorful. This recipe, made with fresh milled corn, will provide you with intensely corn-flavored cornbread.

3 cups all-purpose flour
1 cup yellow cornmeal*
1/4 cup sugar
2 tablespoons baking powder
2 teaspoons kosher salt
2 cups milk
3 extra-large eggs, lightly beaten
1/2 pound unsalted butter, melted,
  plus more as needed
8 ounces aged extra-sharp cheddar cheese, grated
1/3 cup chopped scallions, plus more as needed
3 tablespoons seeded, minced jalapeño peppers

1. In a large bowl, combine the flour, cornmeal, sugar, baking powder and salt.

2. In a separate bowl, combine the milk, eggs and 1/2 pound butter. Stir the wet ingredients into the dry ingredients until well combined and most of the lumps are dissolved.

3. Stir in 2 cups grated cheddar, 1/3 cup scallions and the jalapeños. Allow the mix to sit at room temperature for 20 minutes.

4. Preheat an oven to 350 degrees. Grease a 9-by-13-inch baking pan.

5. Pour the batter into the prepared pan, smoothing the top with a spatula or spoon. Top with the remaining cheddar cheese and chopped scallions, to taste. Bake in the 350-degree oven until a toothpick comes out clean (about 30-35 minutes).

6. Cut into large squares, garnish with more chopped scallions and serve.

*The cornbread pictured was made using white cornmeal instead of yellow cornmeal.

SERVES 12

JEN SHIDELER
HOMETOWN: LOGANSPORT, INDIANA

FROM FIELD TO TABLE. A FAMILY CLASSIC.

SWEET CORN CAKES

BY JEN SHIDELER
(PICTURED ON OPPOSITE PAGE)

THIS IS A WONDERFUL ITEM THAT COULD BE USED as a light dessert or side dish. Traditionally it would be carried by workers as a snack.

1 cup unsalted butter
⅔ cup Masa harina*
½ cup water
1 10-ounce can corn
1 10-ounce can creamed corn
½ cup yellow cornmeal
1 cup sugar, plus more to serve
1 teaspoon baking powder
¼ cup heavy cream
1 teaspoon kosher salt

1. Preheat oven to 350 degrees.

2. In a large bowl, combine the butter, Masa harina and water until well combined. Stir in the creamed and whole kernel corn, and cornmeal.

3. In a separate bowl, combine the sugar, baking powder, salt and cream. Stir into the corn mixture until well combined.

4. Pour the batter into a 8-by-8-inch baking dish and cover with aluminum foil. Bake in the 350-degree oven for 1 hour.

5. Remove from the oven and slice into squares. Sprinkle with sugar and serve.

Masa harina is a very finely ground corn flour made from corn cooked and soaked overnight in limewater, which gives it its distinctive taste. It is traditionally used in Mexican and other Latino dishes to make corn tortillas and tamales.

SERVES 16

CHEDDAR BACON CORNBREAD PIE

BY JENNIFER K. HALLBERG
(PICTURED ABOVE)

Indiana has developed a big following for its cheeses. Capriole goat cheese is world renowned for its silky texture, but the Indiana cheddars are also remarkable.

1 pound bacon
1 cup yellow cornmeal
1 cup milk
2 eggs
½ teaspoon baking soda
1 8-ounce can creamed corn
¾ teaspoon kosher salt
1 cup diced onion
2 cups shredded cheddar cheese

1. Preheat oven to 350 degrees. Lightly grease a 10-inch pie pan.

2. In a skillet over medium-high heat, cook the bacon until it is crisp. Reserve the drippings. Chop the bacon.

3. In a large bowl, combine the cornmeal, milk, eggs, baking soda, creamed corn, salt, onion, bacon and 1 tablespoon of bacon drippings.

4. Pour the corn mixture into the prepared pie pan. Top with the cheddar cheese.

5. Bake uncovered in the 350-degree oven until a toothpick inserted in the center comes out clean (about 50 minutes). If the cheese starts to brown too quickly, cover the pan with aluminum foil.

6. Cut into wedges and serve with chili or a stew.

SERVES 8-10

FOLLOWING HER HEART, AND PALATE

DESSERTS

For Jen Shideler, the kitchen has been her second home. "I have cooked and worked in the food service industry since I was 14," she says. "I didn't realize I wanted to make it a career until I finished college and started working in another field. I realized this is where my heart is, and always has been."

When it came time for the Logansport, Indiana, native to select a program, she chose Ivy Tech Community College based on its impeccable and long-standing reputation, and flexible scheduling. Once enrolled, she discovered the richness of the community. "These chefs really care and impart their passion for food when they teach. We don't just cook, we are challenged to be creative and learn the science behind the dishes."

Shideler, who submitted her take on a family recipe for Sweet Corn Cakes (page 71), plans to graduate from the program in 2009.

MOLLY HARBRIDGE
HOMETOWN: INDIANAPOLIS. INDIANA

SOFTEN EVEN THE TOUGHEST ROAST.

CAJUN COFFEE

BY MOLLY HARBRIDGE
(PICTURED ON OPPOSITE PAGE)

HICKORYWORKS IN SOUTH CENTRAL INDIANA is the only place that makes the shagbark hickory syrup. It is a wonderful sweetener that Hoosiers can call their own. This recipe could also be enlightened with a little bourbon to become a nightcap.

3 cups strong black coffee
¼ cup shagbark hickory syrup
2 teaspoons vanilla extract
Dash ground nutmeg
Dash ground cinnamon, plus more to garnish
1 cup cream, whipped

1. In a large bowl or pitcher, mix together all ingredients except the cream (coffee, syrup, vanilla, nutmeg and cinnamon).
2. Pour into 3 coffee cups. Top each cup with a dollop of whipped cream, dust with cinnamon and serve.

SERVES 3

CINNAMON ROLL MILKSHAKE

BY MOLLY HARBRIDGE
(PICTURED ON PAGE 3)

THIS DESSERT DRINK IS LIKE HAVING BREAKFAST after dinner. Who could resist?

CARAMEL SAUCE

5 tablespoons unsalted butter
1 cup firmly packed brown sugar
¼ cup half-and-half
Pinch kosher salt
½ teaspoon vanilla extract

1. In a saucepot over low heat, melt the butter with the brown sugar.
2. Stir in the half-and-half, salt and vanilla. Bring to a simmer. Remove from heat and reserve for service. Keep at room temperature.

CREAM CHEESE ICING

8 ounces cream cheese
½ cup unsalted butter
3 ¾ cups powdered sugar
1 teaspoon vanilla extract

1. To a large bowl, add all the ingredients. Beat together until smooth.

MILKSHAKE

4 scoops vanilla ice cream
1 3-ounce package vanilla instant pudding, prepared according to package directions
1 cup milk
1 tablespoon shagbark hickory syrup
½ cup crushed walnuts
2 tablespoons Caramel Sauce
Cinnamon-and-sugar mix*
Cream Cheese Icing

1. To a blender, add the ice cream, pudding, milk, syrup, walnuts, caramel sauce and 3 tablespoons cinnamon-and-sugar mix. Blend until smooth.
2. Divide the milkshake among 2 tall glasses. Top with a dollop of cream cheese icing and sprinkle with the remaining cinnamon-and-sugar mix. Serve.

To make cinnamon-and-sugar mix, mix together 3 tablespoons sugar and 2 teaspoons ground cinnamon.

SERVES 2

BLACK WALNUT PRALINES

BY DARCY SMINK
(PICTURED ON OPPOSITE PAGE AND BELOW)

BLACK WALNUT TREES WERE A SIGN TO EARLY AMERICANS that the area was a good place to settle. They grow in naturally fertile lands and are in most areas of Indiana.

2 cups sugar
½ cup firmly packed dark brown sugar
1 cup buttermilk
1 teaspoon baking soda
Pinch kosher salt
4 tablespoons unsalted butter, at room temperature
2 cups black walnut halves, toasted*
1 teaspoon vanilla extract
Vanilla ice cream, to serve (optional)
Melted semisweet chocolate chips,
  to serve (optional)

1. Line a baking sheet with a silicone baking mat or nonstick aluminum foil†.

2. In a large, heavy-bottomed saucepan over low heat, combine the sugars, buttermilk, baking soda and salt. Stir constantly until the sugars dissolve. (If necessary, use a pastry brush dipped in warm water to brush down the sides of the pan.)

3. Cut the butter into small chunks. Add the chunks to the pan, stirring constantly until they are completely melted and incorporated into the sugar mixture.

4. Raise the heat to medium and cook without stirring until the mixture measures 236 degrees on a candy thermometer (soft-ball stage). Remove the pan from the heat and quickly stir in the walnut halves and vanilla extract.

5. Using a wooden spoon, beat the mixture until it becomes thick and opaque (about 1 minute).

6. Using a cookie dough scoop or a tablespoon, drop scoops of the mixture onto the lined baking sheet. Let the pralines cool completely (about 30 minutes).

7. To serve, place 2 pralines on a plate with a side of vanilla ice cream. Or, alternatively, drizzle the pralines with melted semisweet chocolate.

*To toast black walnuts, preheat oven to 350 degrees. Spread the walnuts on a baking sheet and bake in the 350-degree oven for 8-10 minutes, checking frequently to be sure they don't burn.

†If using regular aluminum foil, be sure to brush it lightly with melted butter or coat with nonstick spray.

MAKES 1 ½ POUNDS

DARCY SMINK
HOMETOWN: WEST LAFAYETTE, INDIANA

A FALL TIME ALTERNATIVE FOR THE CANDY DISH.

BITTERSWEET CHOCOLATE PUMPKIN SEED BRITTLE

BY DARCY SMINK
(PICTURED ON OPPOSITE PAGE)

THIS IS A FUN RECIPE TO DO WITH THE KIDS after carving your jack-o'-lanterns in the fall.

2 cups sugar
1 cup light corn syrup
½ cup water
1 cup unsalted butter, cut into chunks,
   plus more as needed
3 cups pumpkin seeds, hulled and toasted*
1 teaspoon baking soda
1 pound bittersweet chocolate, cut into chunks

1. Grease a large baking sheet or jelly roll pan.

2. In a large saucepan, combine the sugar, corn syrup and water. Heat over medium heat, stirring constantly, until the sugar dissolves.

3. Bring the mixture to a boil, and add the butter. Stirring frequently, heat the mixture until it registers 230 degrees on a candy thermometer.

4. Continue cooking until the temperature reaches 280 degrees (soft-crack stage). Add the pumpkin seeds. Stirring constantly, continue to cook until the mixture registers 300 degrees on a candy thermometer (hard-crack stage).

5. Remove from heat and immediately stir in the baking soda. Using a wooden spoon, mix well.

6. Pour the mixture onto the prepared baking sheet. As the candy begins to cool, stretch it out thinner by lifting and pulling at the edges with a fork. Allow the candy to further cool.

7. Meanwhile, in the top of a double boiler over medium heat, melt the chocolate. Remove from heat and allow to cool for 5 minutes.

8. Once slightly cooled, quickly pour the chocolate over the pumpkin seed candy, using a spatula to spread it evenly across the entire candy. (Be careful to do this quickly, or the brittle will soften.) Allow the brittle to cool completely.

9. Once the brittle has completely cooled, break it into bite-size pieces and serve.

*To toast pumpkin seeds, preheat oven to 375 degrees. Toss the pumpkin seeds with 2 tablespoons olive oil and Kosher salt, to taste, until they are well coated. Spread the seeds in a single layer on a baking sheet and bake in the 375-degree oven until they are light brown and crispy (about 7-10 minutes).

MAKES 2 POUNDS

PAUL ROBINSON
HOMETOWN: LAFAYETTE. INDIANA

A CULMINATION OF NEIGHBORING FARE.

OATMEAL RAISIN COOKIE DOUGH FLAUTAS
WITH BOURBON CARAMEL SAUCE

BY PAUL ROBINSON
(PICTURED ON OPPOSITE PAGE)

This recipe combines all the natural goodness of the Midwest. Oatmeal is a wonderful Ohio product, Michigan raisins are some of the best you will ever find, and who could beat the bourbon of Kentucky?

COOKIE DOUGH FLAUTAS

1 ¼ cups unsalted butter
¾ cup brown sugar
½ cup sugar
1 egg
1 teaspoon vanilla extract
1 teaspoon baking soda
1 teaspoon kosher salt
1 teaspoon ground cinnamon
¼ teaspoon ground nutmeg
3 cups old-fashioned rolled oats
1 cup raisins
12 10-inch flour tortillas
Vegetable or canola oil, as needed

BOURBON CARAMEL SAUCE

1 ½ cups brown sugar
1 ½ cups sugar
2 tablespoons all-purpose flour
1 cup water
¼ cup unsalted butter
1 teaspoon vanilla extract
1 tablespoon Sam Cougar bourbon

1. For the cookie dough flautas, in a large bowl, beat together the butter, brown sugar and sugar until fluffy.

2. Add egg and vanilla and beat until well combined.

3. Add the flour, baking soda, salt, cinnamon and nutmeg and mix until well combined.

4. Stir in the oats and raisins until well mixed.

5. Drop 2 tablespoons of the cookie dough into the center of each tortilla. Roll the tortilla up tightly around the dough, forming a long roll.

6. In a large frying pan over high heat, heat the oil. Add the flautas and cook for 2-3 minutes on each side.

7. For the bourbon caramel sauce, in a saucepan over medium heat, combine the brown sugar, sugar, flour and water. Continue to cook over medium heat until the sugars have dissolved and the mixture is clear.

8. Stir in the butter, vanilla and bourbon. Continue to cook over medium heat until the butter is completely melted. Remove from heat.

9. To serve, cut each flauta in half and plate. Drizzle with the warm bourbon caramel sauce.

SERVES 12

A WINTER WARMER WITH THE
FAMILIAR FRUIT OF FALL.

MIDWESTERN APPLE AND CREAM SKILLET SHORTCAKE

BY BRE EINES
(PICTURED ON OPPOSITE PAGE)

THIS IS A GREAT RECIPE TO MAKE IN THE WINTER when you are longing for warmer days. If you have saved apples from a local orchard, this dessert will help bring back thoughts of picking the crop from the trees in October.

2 tablespoons unsalted butter or nonstick
  cooking spray
2 pounds frozen, sliced apples, thawed
½ cup brown sugar
2 teaspoons ground cinnamon
1 teaspoon vanilla extract
2 tablespoons cornstarch
1 8-ounce package cream cheese, chilled and
  cut into ½-inch cubes
¼ cup sugar
1 16.3-ounce can refrigerated biscuits*

1. Preheat oven to 350 degrees. Grease or spray a cast-iron skillet.

2. In a medium bowl, combine the apples, brown sugar, 1 teaspoon cinnamon, vanilla and cornstarch. Mix until the apples are well coated.

3. Pour the apples into the prepared skillet. Top with randomly placed tablespoon-size dollops of cream cheese. Set aside.

4. In a small bowl, combine the sugar and remaining cinnamon. Remove the refrigerated biscuits from the can and separate them. Dredge each biscuit in the cinnamon-sugar mix.

5. Arrange the coated biscuits over the apples in the skillet. Bake in the 350-degree oven until the biscuits are brown and filling is bubbly (about 20-25 minutes).

6. Remove the skillet cake from the oven and allow it to slightly cool before serving.

Chef Eines recommends using Pillsbury brand Grands! Southern Style Biscuits.

SERVES 6-8

JENNIFER K. HALLBERG
HOMETOWN: GOSHEN, INDIANA

PLAYFUL PIES FOR ANY TIME OF DAY.

PUMPKIN SPICE WHOOPIE PIE

BY JENNIFER K. HALLBERG
(PICTURED ON OPPOSITE PAGE)

WHAT A WONDERFUL TREAT. A light pumpkin roll-type cake with marshmallow fluff in the middle.

CAKE

½ cup vegetable shortening
1 cup firmly packed brown sugar
1 cup pureed pumpkin*
1 egg
2 ½ cups all-purpose flour
1 tablespoon ground cinnamon
1 teaspoon baking powder
1 teaspoon baking soda
1 teaspoon kosher salt
1 teaspoon vanilla extract
1 cup milk

FILLING

1 cup unsalted butter, plus more as needed
1 ½ cups powder sugar
2 cups marshmallow fluff
1 ½ teaspoons vanilla extract

1. Preheat oven to 350 degrees. Lightly grease 2 baking sheets.

2. For the cake, in a large bowl, cream together the shortening, brown sugar, pumpkin and egg. Set aside.

3. In a separate large bowl, combine the flour, cinnamon, baking powder, baking soda and salt. Set aside.

4. In a small bowl, stir together the vanilla and milk.

5. Alternate adding the dry ingredients and the vanilla-milk mixture into the shortening mixture, beating after each addition until smooth.

6. Drop the cake batter ¼ cup at a time onto the prepared baking sheets to make 20 cakes. With a spoon, spread the batter into 4-inch circles, leaving about 2 inches in between each cake.

7. Bake in the 350-degree oven until the cakes are firm (about 15 minutes). Remove from the oven and cool on a wire rack.

8. Meanwhile, for the filling, in a large bowl, beat together the butter, sugar and marshmallow until the mixture is smooth. Stir in the vanilla.

9. When the cakes are completely cool, spread a generous amount of filling onto the flat side of 1 cake. Top with another cake to make a sandwich, pressing down gently to even out the filling, and serve.

*To make pureed pumpkin, preheat oven to 325 degrees. Cut the pumpkin in half, stem to base, and remove the seeds and strings. Cover the remaining halves with aluminum foil. Place the pumpkin halves foil side up on a baking sheet and bake in the 325-degree oven until tender (about 1 hour). Remove the pumpkin halves from the oven, scrape out the pumpkin meat and puree the meat in a blender or food processor. Strain before using to remove any remaining strings. Or, for convenience, use a good-quality canned pumpkin puree.

MAKES 10 CAKES

GRAND-MOTHER'S BREAD PUDDING

BY JAMIE MARKS
(PICTURED ON OPPOSITE PAGE)

This is just good ole' Midwest comfort food. When it used to be served with the lemon sauce it was a sign of opulence. Only the very well to do could afford to have citrus and they were sure to serve it at a dinner party.

BREAD PUDDING

5 eggs
3 cups milk
1 cup honey
1 cup half-and-half
¼ cup unsalted butter, melted and cooled
2 teaspoons vanilla extract
1 teaspoon almond extract
½ teaspoon ground nutmeg
4 cups cubed day-old white bread
4 cups cubed day-old wheat bread
⅓ cup raisins

LEMON SAUCE

1½ cups sugar
⅓ cup cornstarch
¼ teaspoon kosher salt
2¼ cups cold water
3 egg yolks, slightly beaten
⅓ cup freshly squeezed lemon juice
2 tablespoons unsalted butter

1. Preheat oven to 350 degrees. Grease a 9-by-13-inch baking dish.

2. For the bread pudding, in a large mixing bowl, combine the eggs, milk, honey, half-and-half, melted butter, vanilla extract, almond extract and ground nutmeg. Stir in the white and wheat bread cubes and the raisins.

3. Transfer the mix to the prepared baking dish and bake, uncovered, for 45-55 minutes.

4. For the lemon sauce, in a large saucepan, combine the sugar, cornstarch, salt and water and mix until they are smooth. Bring the mixture to a boil over medium heat, stirring constantly. Remove from heat.

5. Temper in the egg yolks. To do this, in a heatproof mixing bowl, whisk together the egg yolks. Add a little of the hot sauce to the egg yolks in a steady stream, whisking constantly to keep the yolks from scrambling. Stir the yolks into the remaining sauce in the saucepan.

6. Return the saucepan to the heat. Stirring constantly, bring to a gentle boil. Cook and stir for an additional 2 minutes. Remove from the heat and gently stir in the lemon juice and butter.

7. To serve, plate the warm bread pudding and top with the lemon sauce.

SERVES 12-15

SWEET POTATO CHEESECAKE

BY JENNIFER K. HALLBERG
(PICTURED BELOW, LEFT)

THIS IS A PLAYFUL TWIST ON THE CANDIED SWEET POTATOES we all have at Thanksgiving.

CRUST

1 1/2 cups graham cracker crumbs
1/2 cup finely chopped walnuts
6 tablespoons unsalted butter, melted

FILLING

8 ounces cream cheese, softened
4 ounces (1/2 cup) sugar
4 ounces (1/2 cup) dark brown sugar
1 teaspoon ground cinnamon
1/2 teaspoon ground ginger
1/2 teaspoon ground nutmeg
8 ounces pureed sweet potatoes*
5 eggs
1/2 cup heavy cream
2 cups mini marshmallows

1. Preheat oven to 350 degrees.

2. For the crust, in a medium bowl, combine the graham cracker crumbs, walnuts and butter. Press the mixture into a 9-inch springform pan and set aside.

3. For the filling, in the bowl of a stand mixer, beat the cream cheese until smooth. Add the sugars, cinnamon, ginger and nutmeg and beat until light and fluffy (about 3 minutes). Add the sweet potato puree and mix until just blended.

4. Add in the eggs one at a time, beating between each addition until fully incorporated and stopping to scrape down the bowl as needed. Stir in the heavy cream and mix until it is fully incorporated.

5. Pour the filling into the crust. Place the springform pan in a larger rimmed baking pan and fill with water to create a 1-inch-deep water bath. Bake the cheesecake in the 350-degree oven for 50 minutes.

6. Remove from the oven and top the cheesecake with the marshmallows. Return the cheesecake to the oven and continue to bake until the marshmallows are melted and toasted on top (about 10 minutes).

7. Let the cheesecake cool at room temperature for 45 minutes and then chill in the refrigerator for at least 4 hours before service.

*To make sweet potato puree, preheat oven to 375 degrees. Using a fork, prick 1-2 sweet potatoes on all sides. Place on a baking sheet and bake in the 375-degree oven until tender (about 1 hour). Remove from the oven and allow the sweet potatoes to cool. Once they are cool enough to handle, peel them with a vegetable peeler and cut the potatoes into small pieces. Place the pieces in the bowl of a food processor and puree, adding water as needed to achieve a smooth consistency. You could also use canned yams and puree them in a food processor or blender.

MAKES 1 CHEESECAKE, SERVES 8

LARRY'S FAVORITE SHOOFLY PIE

BY DARCY SMINK
(PICTURED BELOW, RIGHT)

SHOOFLY PIE IS A PENNSYLVANIA DISH that was popularized by the Amish. It is a rich decadent pie that cries out for a good cup of coffee to match.

PIE CRUST

¾ cup cake flour
½ cup all-purpose flour
1 tablespoon sugar
½ teaspoon kosher salt
7 tablespoons vegetable shortening, chilled and cut into small pieces
4 tablespoons ice water

TOPPING

⅔ cup firmly packed light brown sugar
½ cup all-purpose flour
1½ teaspoons ground cinnamon
½ teaspoon grated nutmeg
¼ cup unsalted butter, softened

FILLING

½ teaspoon baking soda
1 cup warm water
2 large eggs
½ cup light corn syrup
½ cup sorghum*
1 cup bittersweet chocolate chips
Whipped cream, to serve
Unsweetened Dutch-process cocoa powder, to garnish

1. For the pie crust, in a large bowl, combine the flours, sugar and salt. Using a pastry fork or blender, add the cold shortening. Blend until well combined and the mixture resembles coarse crumbs.

2. Add the ice water one tablespoon at a time, mixing after each addition, until the dough begins to stick together. (You may not need to use all the ice water). Press the dough into a ball.

3. Flatten the dough into a disk and wrap it in plastic wrap. Chill in the refrigerator until the dough is firm (about 20 minutes).

4. Preheat oven to 400 degrees.

5. Remove the dough from the refrigerator. On a floured work surface, roll the dough out into an 11-inch circle. Line a 9-inch pie pan with the dough, trimming and crimping the edges to form a crust. Set aside.

6. For the Topping, in a small mixing bowl, combine all ingredients (brown sugar, flour, cinnamon, nutmeg and butter). Using your fingers, mix until well combined and there are no large chunks of butter. Set aside.

7. For the Filling, in a small bowl, whisk together the baking soda and water until well blended.

8. In a separate bowl, whisk together the eggs, corn syrup and sorghum until well combined.

9. Sprinkle the chocolate chips evenly over the bottom of the pie shell. Pour the filling over the chocolate chips, and then top with one-third of the topping mixture.

10. Place the pie on a baking sheet and bake in the 400-degree oven for 25 minutes.

11. Remove the pie from the oven and sprinkle with the remaining topping mixture. Return the pie to the oven and bake until browned and bubbling (about 5 more minutes).

12. Remove pie from the oven and cut into 8 slices. Top with a dollop of whipped cream, dust with unsweetened Dutch-process cocoa powder and serve warm or at room temperature.

*Chef Smink prefers to use Gold Run brand sorghum.

SERVES 8

JENNIFER K. HALLBERG
HOMETOWN: GOSHEN, INDIANA

THIS RICH FINALE SCREAMS FOR MILK.

PEANUT BUTTER BROWNIE PIE

BY JENNIFER K. HALLBERG
(PICTURED ON OPPOSITE PAGE)

JENNIFER'S PIE BRINGS TO MIND all of the wonderful brownies and fudges that are available through Nashville, Indiana.

1 cup peanut butter of choice
½ cup milk
1 pint heavy cream
1½ cups sugar
1 cup unsalted butter, melted, plus more as needed
2/3 cup unsweetened cocoa powder
3 eggs
1½ teaspoons vanilla extract
6 tablespoons all-purpose flour,
  plus more as needed
2 teaspoons baking powder
Vanilla ice cream, to serve

1. Preheat oven to 325 degrees. Grease and flour a 10-inch pie pan.

2. To a large bowl, add the peanut butter and the milk and beat until smooth and creamy.

3. To a separate large bowl, add the heavy cream and ½ cup sugar. Beat until moderately stiff peaks form.

4. Fold the whipped cream into the peanut butter mixture. Set aside.

5. In a large bowl, combine the butter, cocoa and the remaining 1 cup sugar until well combined. Add the eggs one at a time, mixing well after each addition to be sure it is fully incorporated.

6. Stir in the vanilla, flour and baking powder.

7. Pour half of the brownie mixture into the prepared pie pan. Top with the peanut butter mixture and then pour the remaining brownie mixture on top of that. Bake in the 325-degree oven until the brownie starts to pull away from the sides of the pan (about 30 minutes).

8. Remove from the oven and let cool for 5 minutes before slicing. Serve with a scoop of vanilla ice cream.

SERVES 8

JOEL RIFKIND, DDS
HOMETOWN: INDIANAPOLIS, INDIANA

BOLD CHERRIES ARE A PERFECT ACCESSORY.

CHERRY AND ALMOND RICE PUDDING

BY JOEL RIFKIND, DDS
(PICTURED ON OPPOSITE PAGE)

WHEN I WAS A KID I remember my mom making a similar dish. It was a treat we shared after we had collected the cherries off of the tree in the backyard.

3 cups milk
½ cup plus 1 tablespoon sugar
¼ teaspoon kosher salt
½ cup rice
1 cup red sour cherries, fresh or frozen and thawed
1 tablespoon unsalted butter
1 teaspoon almond extract
½ teaspoon ground cinnamon
½ cup slivered blanched almonds, to garnish
Freshly grated nutmeg, to garnish

1. In a pot over medium heat, combine the milk, ½ cup sugar and salt. Heat until small bubbles begin to form around the edges of the pan.

2. Stir in the rice. Cover the pot, reduce the heat to low and cook over low heat, stirring occasionally, until the rice is tender and most of the liquid is absorbed (about 35-45 minutes).

3. Stir in the cherries, butter and almond extract. Remove from heat.

4. In a small bowl, combine the remaining 1 tablespoon sugar with the cinnamon.

5. To serve, spoon the rice pudding into bowls. Sprinkle with the cinnamon-sugar mix and garnish with almond slivers and nutmeg, to taste.

SERVES 4

INDEX